Criminal Justice
Recent Scholarship

Edited by
Nicholas P. Lovrich

A Series from LFB Scholarly

Cyberbullying
Causes, Consequences, and Coping Strategies

Nicole L. Weber and William V. Pelfrey, Jr.

LFB Scholarly Publishing LLC
El Paso 2014

Library of Congress Cataloging-in-Publication Data

Library of Congress Cataloging-in-Publication Data

Weber, Nicole L.
Cyberbullying : causes, consequences, and coping strategies / Nicole L. Weber and William V. Pelfrey, Jr.
pages cm
Includes bibliographical references and index.
ISBN 978-1-59332-761-3 (hardcover : alk. paper)
1. Cyberbullying. 2. Bullying in schools. 3. Computer crimes. 4. Internet and teenagers. I. Title.
LB3013.3.W44 2014
371.7'82--dc23
2014019397

ISBN 978-1-59332-761-3

Manufactured in the United States of America.

Table of Contents

Acknowledgements

The authors would first like to thank the students, teachers, and administrative staff that participated in this research. Without their thoughtful observations this study would not have been possible.

Portions of this research were supported by a federal grant, jointly sponsored by the Departments of Education, Justice, and Labor through the *Safe Schools/Healthy Students Program*.

We would like to thank our colleagues who participated, advised, and facilitated these research efforts—especially Raji Swaminathan for her thoughtful insight during the design, collection, and analysis phases of this study.

We would also like to express our gratitude to LFB Publishing for their careful review and guidance during the editing phase.

Finally, the authors gratefully acknowledge the support, sacrifice, and inspiration of our spouses and children. We hope that these findings will inform school systems and decision makers, thereby benefiting children like Riley, Lulu, Max, and Kat in the future.

CHAPTER 1

Teen Technology Use and Cyberbullying

John Halligan writes in Kowalski, Limber, and Agatston's (2008) book, Cyber Bullying: Bullying in the Digital Age:

> October 7, 2003, will always be the day that divides my life. Before that day, my son Ryan was alive. A sweet, gentle, and lanky 13-year-old fumbling his way through early adolescence and trying to establish his place in the often confusing and difficult social world of middle school. After that day, my son would be gone forever. A death by suicide. Some would call it bullycide or even cyber bullycide. I just call it a huge hole in my heart that will never heal ... My son was an early casualty and his death an early warning to our society that we'd better pay close attention to how our children use technology. We need to study this new societal problem with a sense of urgency and great diligence. (p. ix-xi)

Advancements in social technologies are currently changing our everyday experiences as they allow us to extend our network of relationships to a world that is accessible with a mere click of the mouse or swipe of a screen 24 hours a day, 7 days a week. These advancements are profoundly transforming how we work, learn, and communicate with one another. In the workplace we rely on the Internet to connect us to the latest information, as well as communicate and collaborate with fellow workers via email, instant messengers, and video conferencing. Scholars use electronic databases to conduct research and utilize learning management systems to teach and take courses online. Socially, we use communicative platforms (e.g., Google Chat, Skype, email) and social networking sites (i.e., Facebook, Twitter, Instagram) to connect with colleagues, friends, and family members. We snap pictures and record videos with our cell phones for upload to YouTube or Facebook to share with not only our world, but *the* world. Social technology is now seen as a seamless addendum to our daily lives (North, Snyder, & Bulfin, 2008).

TEEN SOCIAL TECHNOLOGY USE

While technological advancements are currently transforming the world for persons of all ages, we have chosen to focus on teenagers for this study. This population has the greatest access to computers and the Internet of any generation (Watkins, 2009). Further, they are the first generation to have significant access to cell phones at an early age, which gives them access "on the go" to the Internet and to their social peer networks. Youth are avid early adopters of technology (Ito et al., 2010) who integrate different kinds of technology seamlessly into their lives (boyd, 2008) by fluidly layering social media in a multitasking, multi-screen world (boyd, 2007d; digital_nation, 2010; Ito et al., 2010; Watkins, 2009). This means that teens are not only using communication technology but also using multiple forms of that technology at once in a natural way for entertainment, the communication of messages to others, and learning opportunities soon after they emerge on the scene. These technologies are being embraced at younger ages and even becoming a dominant medium for communication between youth peer networks (Mishna, Saini, & Solomon, 2009). Not only are children familiar with such technology by the time they become teenagers, but a majority of them have their own cell phones and home Internet access (Agatston, Kowalski, & Limber, 2007)—sometimes even available from the privacy of their own rooms.

Cell phones and different forms of computer-mediated communication tools give teenagers many options to connect with their peer networks. Cell phones now give individuals access to their social peer networks through voice calling, texting, and the Internet by way of their carrier or a public connection (e.g., Wi-Fi). This access grants individuals a constant and consistent communication channel to their friends, favorite Internet sites, and social networking sites. Cell phones, now ubiquitous among teenagers, have become a virtual necessity to navigating their world.

Access to the Internet can open a world of options for communicating with others. Websites often have message board or comment options, which allow individuals to post their ideas and feelings on an array of topics, videos, or current event issues. Blogs allow the option to have a whole website based on your thoughts, dedicated to a specific—or even a broad—topic area. Email allows for asynchronous communication between individuals, which provides time to develop and edit communiqués. Instant messaging systems make it possible to chat with friends in a synchronous, real-time manner, using written text under the radar of others (e.g., parents) that might be observing. Social networking sites like Facebook provide forums for many of these communication pathways in a single venue. On Facebook individuals can create a profile of information about themselves that others can see, post public or private messages asynchronously to friends, synchronously chat with friends, indicate up-to-date happenings via status messages, and share their latest pictures, videos, and links to newsworthy or entertainment material.

Contemporary youth have access to the tools necessary to communicate in these fashions and utilize them to interact in many different ways. As described in Table 1, a majority of teenagers have a cell phone and access to a computer, with almost a quarter indicating ownership of a tablet (Madden, Lenhart, Duggan, Cortesi, & Gasser, 2013).

Table 1: *Youth Access to Technology*

Technology	Access %
Cell Phone	78%
Tablet	23%
In-Home Computer Access	93%

Madden et al. (2013) also highlight the increasing use of smartphones and other mobile devices among teenagers. According to their report, 74% of teens indicated they accessed the Internet on their cell phones, tablets, and other mobile devices. Further, "one in four teens are 'cell-mostly' internet users, who say they primarily go online using their phone and not using some other device such as a desktop or laptop computer" (Madden et al., 2013, p. 2). This access gives youth a consistent access to their peers.

Replication of Peer Networks

While social technology has the ability to connect individuals to the larger world, people tend to stick to their established physical networks (boyd, 2008; Ito et al., 2010). For the average teenager, educational experiences are the center of life, as they comprise a majority of their daily interactions. Often, these experiences vary by gender, race, ethnicity, immigrant status, English proficiency, and family socioeconomic background. Peer interaction in schools shapes peer network composition, as well as how these networks function. Much of the peer interaction in schools occurs in unstructured and mostly unsupervised spaces like hallways, bathrooms, and lunchrooms. Social technology, like social networking sites and using electronic devices to communicate, has become widespread among youth and can extend these unstructured and unsupervised spaces. Thus, it is important to explore how environments supported by social technology impact teenagers, as well as how it influences the way they interact with one another in their peer networks.

Cyberbullying Perpetration and Victimization

Initial research has shown that teenagers use social technology in an "always-on" (Ito et al., 2010) capacity which extends the ability to connect with friends, make social plans, and support one another when there is a physical space between them (Juvonen & Gross, 2008; Lenhart, Madden, Macgill, & Smith, 2007; Subrahmanyam & Greenfield, 2008). It also allows them the opportunity to negotiate identity (boyd & Ellison, 2007) while passing time with different entertainment venues such as surfing friends' and friends' of friends profiles and watching friends' links to videos (boyd, 2007b; Lenhart, et al., 2007).

While social technology provides a space for friends to close the after school physical distance it can unfortunately become a space to spread rumors and socially sabotage peers by inflicting fear, helplessness, and humiliation (Hinduja & Patchin, 2009; Mason, 2008; Strom & Strom, 2005). Thus, it is important to understand the nature and extent of cyberbullying and cybervictimization among teenagers who share the same school environment. Few empirical studies (Agatston, Kowalski, & Limber, 2007; Allen, 2012; Hinduja & Patchin, 2007; Hinduja & Patchin, 2008; Hinduja & Patchin, 2010a; Hinduja &

Patchin, 2010b; Hinduja & Patchin, 2013; Kowalski, Morgan, & Limber, 2012; Mishna, Saini, & Solomon, 2009; Patchin & Hinduja, 2006; Raskauskas & Stoltz, 2007; Vandebosch & Van Cleemput, 2008; Varjas, Henrich, & Meyers, 2009; Williams & Guerra, 2007) have been conducted on cyberbullying in the United States, and many of these have generated inconclusive or contradictory results.

Researchers have reported cyberbullying victimization rates ranging from 11% (Kowalski & Limber, 2007) of participating students being cyberbullied over the past few months to 72% (Juvonen & Gross, 2008) reporting at least one online incident of bullying. Some studies have hinted at relationships between cyberbullying and engaging in risky behaviors such as drinking alcohol and cigarette use (Bailey, 2008; Hinduja & Patchin, 2009; Hinduja & Patchin, 2007; Mason, 2008; McGuinness, 2007; Patchin & Hinduja, 2006). Some researchers have also found links between time spent online and cyberbullying engagement (Hinduja & Patchin 2007; Hinduja & Patchin 2009; Smith et al., 2008) but found inconclusive support of significant relationships to demographic variables linked to race, class, and gender (Dempsey, Sulkowski, Nichols, & Storch, 2009; Hinduja & Patchin, 2009; Li, 2006; Li, 2007). Hinduja and Patchin (2007) found that age and cyberbullying were significant and that older youth were engaged in more problem behaviors whereas Varjas et al., (2009) found that older students reported less physical, verbal, and relational victimization, and less physical and verbal bullying. Further, Varjas et al., (2009) found that students did not equate a decrease in school safety to acts of cyberbullying.

Cyberbullying is occurring but conclusive evidence of relationships within the phenomenon does not currently exist. There are deficits in the current literature concerning definitions of cyberbullying, cyberbullying victimization and perpetration rates, the influence of demographic variables (e.g., race, gender, social class, etc.) on cyberbullying incidence, and the relationship between cyberbullying and risky behaviors. Thus, there is a significant deficit in the current education, criminal justice, and public health literatures that needs to address how cyberbullying extends to school.

The extant study examines how peer networks extend from the school day to social technology and back to school. Further, this research focuses on cyberbullying incidence (i.e., rate of occurrence), characteristics of victimization (i.e., being cyberbullied) and perpetration (i.e., committing cyberbullying acts), as well as impact featuring potential relationships with school violence, teenage suicide, and risky behaviors (e.g., smoking cigarettes, drinking alcohol, and taking drugs). These acts and relationships have the potential to affect schools and have consequences that could influence students well past their schooling years.

Definition of Key Terms

It is important to document a few integral terminology choices for this particular project. In this section we make use of the terms social technology, teenagers, social network[ing], friends, peer networks, and cyberbullying.

Social Technology vs. Social Media

In this study we will refer to things like texting, YouTube, social networks, email, and instant messaging as *social technology*. Many researchers in the field are referring to items such as YouTube and social networks as social media but definitions around this specific term are not yet clear. Bradley (2010) calls for a clearer definition in the field and indicates that "at its foundation, social media is a set of technologies and channels targeted at forming and enabling a potentially massive community of participants to productively collaborate" ("A New Definition of Social Media," 2010). Thus, a major component of social media comes in the form of the inherent features that focus on interaction between and among community members.

Nations (n.d.) defines the term by breaking it down, indicating that media are instruments of communication, such as newspapers and the radio. Thus Nations (n.d.) agrees with Bradley (2010) in that social media are social instruments of communication where information is shared and interaction takes place. While this is true, the term social media in other definitions seems to focus on things such as social bookmarking, social photo sharing, social video sharing, and other forms of user-generated content (Bian, Agichtein, Liu, & Zha, 2008) and not on other forms of communication tools that individuals use to interact with one another such as cell phones, texting, and instant messaging when all these tools are used to facilitate interaction and communication-sharing. While we agree that social media do feature interaction around media items—such as videos and current events—which is important in this study, we feel that the term media is too restricting as it fails to incorporate some of the tools and actions (i.e., cell phones and texting) which teens are using the most. Thus, we feel that the more encompassing term *social technology* is a more appropriate as it includes these other forms of communication tools for this particular study.

Teenagers

This study will refer to middle and high school students as "teenagers." Youth will also be used interchangeably. The Pew Research Center's American Life Project refers to all individuals 12-17 as teenagers in their several distributed reports (e.g., Lenhart, Ling, Campbell, and Purcell, 2010; Lenhart, Purcell, Smith, & Zickuhr, 2010; Madden et al., 2013). Because we will be referring to this study when we discuss current literature, we feel it is appropriate to refer to middle and high school students in this study in the same manner. While those 12-year-old individuals are technically pre-teenagers, they have been shown in these reports to have the same basic technology use patterns as their fully teenage counterparts making the more inclusive "teenage" term work well for this set of participants.

Social Network vs. Social Networking

Up until this point we have used social networking because that is the term with which most are familiar when referring to these kinds of sites. However, for the rest of this book we will refer to social networking sites as social network sites. The conscious decision to drop the "ing" ending reflects the idea that individuals typically make connections with those with whom they already have some kind of connection. Convoluted ideas exist of what the Internet and social network environments represent. When people write about the benefits of these phenomena they typically speak to the idea of opening up worlds of knowledge and creating new connections with people from other places and cultures. While they most certainly have the potential to do that, they are mostly utilized to attain goals that reside in a person's immediate world. Further, "social networking" implies the creation of a new relationship, which has not typically been the main use of these sites (boyd & Ellison, 2007). This does not, however, insinuate that these sites do not make a difference in people's lives, because they most clearly have done so. Instead of forging new relationships, however, they typically build existing ones that may not have flourished without the existence of these sites through their social interaction and information distribution (boyd, 2007a).

"Friends" and "Buddies"

In social network environments, when a social connection has been extended and accepted between individuals the connection is denoted as being one among "friends." The same can be said in instant messaging programs where these connections in some programs are also referred to as friends (e.g., Yahoo! Messenger) and others "buddies" (e.g., AOL Instant Messenger, iChat). One of the most important things to realize about networked environments and the social technology tools used to access these environments is that they revolve around the idea of creating identity, as well as making connections and fostering interactions with these "friends" or "buddies." Now, these "friends" are not always necessarily true friends. As we know from our physical, face-to-face world "friends" are not always friend-friends; when we try to categorize who is what, it can get quite complex. We have work friends, close friends, high school friends, college friends, friends of friends, and the list could go on. The same can be said for our virtual world as we often put forth and accept connections to individuals we may not have strong connections to, persons we only partially know or know by way of an acquaintance. Thus, it is important to understand that things that are done on social network sites have a veiled visibility as they are done in front of our audience of "friends" without physically seeing them and possibly without recollection of who that audience may include. However, it is necessary to recognize that our face-to-face physical worlds overlap with our virtual worlds through our peer networks.

Virtual and Face-to-Face Peer Networks

For this project we investigate the overlap between virtual and face-to-face peer middle and high school networks. Porter (2004) defines virtual communities as "an aggregation of individuals or business partners who interact around a shared interest, where the interaction is at least partially supported and/or mediated by technology and guided by some protocols or norms" (Introduction section, para. 7). In the case of this study the shared interest is the perpetuation of the daily lives where middle and high school students use social technology to extend their school face-to-face peer networks in a virtual manner. Participation does not have to be limited to an either-or situation—individuals can and do participate in the same peer network both physically and virtually (Wellman et al., 1996). Researcher boyd (2008), through her studies, demonstrates that this is very much the case—that is, teenagers are typically using things such as social network sites, instant messaging, and texting to keep in touch with their school peer networks. She observes that only in the cases of marginalization are they motivated to seek the networks of pure strangers.

Cyberbullying vs. Harassment

Currently the field is going through conceptualization issues when it comes to defining what exactly cyberbullying is, and what it is not. This lack of consensus will be depicted more fully in the next chapter. However, for this study cyberbullying will be defined as "an aggressive, intentional act carried out by a group or an individual, using electronic forms of contact, repeatedly and over time against a victim who can not easily defend him or herself" (Dooley, Pyzalski, & Cross, 2009 as cited in Smith et al., 2008, p. 182) from a bully of the same age that exerts his/her power. We have chosen this definition because it depicts cyberbullying as an aggressive, intentional, and repeated act that is produced by an individual of the same age group that exerts his/her power over a victim that can not easily defend her/himself though an electronic medium featuring social technology tools such as instant messaging, email, texting, and social network sites.

Some researchers have called cyberbullying behavior harassment, or grouped it into the category of online victimization. It is differentiated from normal harassment because harassment typically entails an age differential—underage vs. over age—between the victim and the perpetrator (WiredKids, nd). Early research (Mitchell, Finkelhor, & Wolak, 2004) in the field referred to this phenomenon as online victimization, a category of behavior which included everything from sexual solicitation to online bullying behaviors. Around this time Ybarra and Mitchell (2004) started to use the term Internet harassment, which they define to involve "an overt, intentional act of aggression towards another person online" (p. 1308).

Wolak, Mitchell, and Finkelhor (2007) delve into this choice of terminology a little more as they prefer Internet or online harassment because that behavior "does not constitute bullying unless it is related to offline bullying" (p. S57) as it does not always meet the traditional bullying classification of aggression, repetition, and power imbalance. While we agree with this observation to an extent, we do not want to trivialize online harassment when the perpetrator is not known, or if known is a relative stranger because behaviors can be equally troubling to the victim given the circumstance, and one of our main concerns should be victim impact. Due to the overlap of face-to-face peer networks and virtual networks, as well as recent researchers discussing how bullying via online means can incorporate aggression, repetition, and power imbalance this study utilizes the *cyberbullying* term.

Chapter Summary

While recent media coverage has provided general public awareness of cyberbullying, further study is needed to examine the relationships that exist within the phenomenon. Subsequent chapters will present a detailed review of extant literature and the research methodology that guides this study. John Halligan and other parents who have had to come to terms with the suicides of their children understand the importance of further study on the cyberbullying phenomenon. Cyberbullying is occurring through social technology. An understanding is needed regarding how and why cyberbullying occurs and which relationships predict participation in cyberbullying activity. Thus, it is necessary to conduct qualitative, quantitative, and mixed methods studies, which enhance understanding of the cyberbullying phenomenon and inform intervention and prevention programs.

CHAPTER 2

Teen Technology Use, Bullying, and Cyberbullying Literature

> "...understanding an individual's technological environment is now a vital clue in understanding how that person uses the Internet, connects with others, and accesses information" (Lenhart, Purcell, Smith, & Zickuhr, 2010, p. 9).

Bullying is currently being extended by advancements in technology. With a majority of our nation's youth participating in social network sites and other forms of social technology, researchers must move past the novelty of the new technology and move towards empirical study regarding the impact of its use on students and school environments. Social technology provides students with a 24-hour a day, 7-day a week access to their personal, physical face-to-face networks. While this can be beneficial for youngsters struggling through "growing pains" as social technology can extend supportive peer networks, there are negative implications such as cyberbullying, where unflattering pictures, rumors, and messages can be widely and quickly distributed. This is especially relevant in the current school climate as there is a heightened concern over students committing violent acts against other students and self-destructive acts against themselves. Researchers must therefore construct an understanding of bullying that begins in cyberspace and determine whether that behavior contributes to school violence, teenage suicide, and participation in risky behaviors such as smoking cigarettes, drinking alcohol, and taking drugs.

This review of scholarly literature is broken into four major sections: *teen social technology use*, *social technology use and peer interactions*, *bullying*, and *cyberbullying*. Teen social technology use will specifically explore which tools teens are utilizing and focus on what teens use these tools for, as well as usage differences by demographics. Social technology use and peer interactions will examine technology as an agent of fostering teen interactions by looking at them as an addendum to peer culture and follow with the potential benefits and harms to youth who participate in these environments. As cyberbullying is an emerging field, it is necessary to review related traditional bullying literature before exploring the current field of cyberbullying. The final section of this review conveys the conceptualization of cyberbullying, current cyberbullying studies, cyberbullying's connection to traditional bullying, and bullying and cyberbullying's connection to risky offline behaviors.

TEEN SOCIAL TECHNOLOGY USE

Before discussing how social technology is working to affect peer interaction and how that may influence cyberbullying activity, it is important to first understand the tools teenagers are using to communicate with one another. Lenhart, Purcell, Smith, and Zickuhr (2010) observe that "understanding an individual's technological environment is now a vital clue in understanding how that person uses the Internet, connects with others, and accesses information" (p. 9). Therefore, it is important for this study to grasp teens' worlds and how the different aspects of them interact when connecting with one another and accessing information virtually, as well as face-to-face. For this purpose, we will utilize recent statistics, which were released in reports by Lenhart et al. (2010), Lenhart, Ling, Campbell, and Purcell (2010), and Madden et al. (2013) as part of the latest research projects regarding teens and technology use by the PEW Research Center's Internet and American Life Project. These reports are based on information collected from a nationally representative sample of teens aged 12-17 and their parents by way of a telephone survey.

Forms of Technology Teens Use to Connect with Each Other

According to Lenhart, Purcell, Smith, and Zickuhr (2010) 93% of teens aged12-17 go online, with 63% going online once a day and 36% going online several times a day. Lenhart, Purcell, Smith, and Zickuhr (2010) indicate that laptops are now the computer of choice of those under 30. While not overtly stated in the report, this is most likely due to the portability of laptops over the conventional traditional desktop computers. Thus, teens can take laptops into the privacy of their own rooms, as well as to school, to their friends' houses, and other public venues.

During the survey teens were asked which of the following "gadgets" they currently owned: cell phone, MP3 player, computer, game consoles, and/or portable gaming devices. Responses indicate that the average rate of possession of these items is 3.5/5. Lenhart, Purcell, Smith, and Zickuhr (2010) indicate that 80% of teens have gaming systems and 75% of teens have cell phones. Further, new technology items such as gaming systems and cell phones "provide new ways for teens…to go online" (p.13) to connect with each other and access information.

However, cell phones are used for much more than just accessing online venues. According to Lenhart, Ling, Campbell, and Purcell (2010) cell phones are utilized by teens for a number of functions. These reasons are illustrated in Table 2.

Table 2: ***Cell Phone Functions***

Cell Phone Feature	Use %
Taking Pictures	83%
Share Pictures	64%
Listen to Music	60%
Play Games	46%
Exchange Videos	32%
Instant Message	31%
Go Online	27%
Access Social Networks	23%
Email	21%

While teens use these cell phone features to connect and share information with one another, they also use their cell phone for text messaging and "old-fashioned" calling. Lenhart, Ling, Campbell, and Purcell (2010) indicate that "texting has overtaken the frequency of every other common form of interaction" for teenagers (p. 2). They support this statement with their finding that 72% of all teens are text-messengers. Further, one third of teens send more than 100 texts a day or more than 3,000 texts a month.

Interestingly, the study found that 58% of cell-owning teens who attended schools which banned cell phones reported sending texts while class was being conducted. This means that many students—even when prohibited by schools—are still motivated to bring these devices into school and interact with their contacts. These researchers make it clear that while texting is the most common function of cell phone use, calling is still a central cell phone function for most teenagers and that the mobile phone is increasingly important for connecting with others.

Teens are going online, connecting with one another in many different ways, and using many different tools to do so. Social network usage is a key element of teenage online activity. Lenhart, Purcell, Smith, and Zickuhr (2010) report that 73% of teenagers are currently using social networking sites. This represents an increase from 65% in 2008 and 55% in 2006. They found teens that go online daily are more likely to make use of social network systems, utilizing different aspects of the sites. Even though there has been a slight decline in some activity, 50% of teens still send group messages and 66% send private messages to their friends. The most common activities are posting and commenting on pictures, sending instant messages through the chat features, and commenting on the public wall profile spaces.

These researchers also found that blogging interest in general is down. Nearly 28% participated in blogging activities in 2006, but now that figure has decreased to 14%. On the other hand, using these tools for entertainment purposes—such as playing games, visiting websites (e.g., sports, music, etc.), photo-sharing (e.g., Flickr), and video-sharing (e.g., YouTube)—are quite popular among teens (Lenhart, Ling, Campbell, & Purcell, 2010). Further, teens tend to use these tools to visit websites around current events and politics, buy things, and learn about topics they might not feel comfortable discussing with others—such as heath, fitness, and sexual activity.

Teen technology use has become highly mobile, predicated upon cell phones, tablets, and laptops. A number of recent reports by the Pew Research Center's *Internet and American Life Project* describe social technology use by teenagers. Madden et al (2013), in *Teens and Technology 2013,* document the use of technology by teenagers to communicate with one another. According to this study a majority of teenagers had access to a cell phone (78%) and an in-home computer (93%) with almost a quarter (23%) indicating ownership of a tablet. Further, 74% of teens indicated that accessed the Internet on their cell phones, tablets, and other mobile devices. One in four teens in this study showed a preference for being "cell-mostly" Internet users indicating that they mostly went online using their phone instead of a desktop or laptop computer. With teenagers having access to the tools necessary (e.g., cell phones, laptops, tablets, etc.) it is important to note that nearly all (95%) teens are online and a majority (80%) of them are users of social network sites (Madden et al., 2013).

Knowing that many teens are online, communicating with each other in diverse ways, and using the different tools available to them to connect with others and entertain themselves, it is important to consider on the influence of demographic characteristics.

Demographics and Social Technology Use

Lenhart, Purcell, Smith, and Zickuhr (2010) found that 75% of teenagers have cell phones and they described usage based on age, race, gender, and socioeconomic status. Cell phone use increases with age; they found that 58% of 12 year olds had cell phones, while 73% of 13 year olds and 83% of 17 year olds did. While the survey data did not qualitatively measure why these differences exist, it may be due to access milestones (e.g., a certain birthday, entering high school, etc.) instituted by parents. Further, they found cell phone use to cut across demographic groups, with both boys and girls equally likely to have them and there to be no significant differences in access by race and ethnicity. Researchers found that socioeconomic status plays a role in cell phone ownership as low income families were less likely to have teens with cell phones.

Although cell phones have helped close the digital divide, Lenhart, Ling, Campbell, and Purcell (2010) note that the cost of cell phones and plans preclude lower income families, and teens, from ownership. They found that sex plays a role in cell phone usage. Boys typically send 30 texts per day while girls send more—around 80 per day. Texting also differed by age, with 12-13 year olds only sending 20 per day and 14-17 year olds sending 60 per day. The most active texters were girls 14-17 as they sent an average of 100 texts per day (Lenhart, Ling, Campbell, & Purcell, 2010).

Both boys and girls are equally likely to go online (Lenhart, Purcell, Smith, & Zickuhr, 2010). Younger teens, aged 12-13 (88%), were less likely than older teens 14-17 (95%) to go online. Older teens not only went online more frequently, they go online several times a day more than their younger counterparts. This report indicates that broadband access is becoming the norm for many families as 76% of families with a 12-17 year old had this advanced access. Teens that had access to a home broadband connection (40%) went online more frequently than those with the cheaper dial-up access (21%). Another important aspect of computer usage and accessing online venues is computer ownership. A majority (69%) of those 12-17 had computers, with wealthier families more likely to have teenagers who have their own computers. Computer ownership rates increase with parental educational attainment and familial income.

Summary: Teen Technology Use

Teenagers own many different kinds of gadgets (e.g., cell phones, laptops, iPods, game consoles, portable gaming devices) which provide a constant connectivity to the Internet and their friends. They connect with their peers to share pictures, exchange videos, access social network sites, and relay information via things such as texting and instant messaging. While the digital divide is being bridged by the different tools available to individuals at increasingly affordable rates, some differences still exist in the participatory divide between those that have higher familial income and parental educational attainment as those assets afford teenagers access at difference paces. There are substantial differences in access. Slower Internet connections decreases motivation and changes the way Internet-based tools are used. There are also differences in Internet access by device (e.g., cell phone vs. laptop) as websites work to become more mobile-friendly and by public connection (e.g., Wi-Fi) with teenagers connecting to the Internet in public spaces like coffee shops, restaurants, and libraries.

It is important to note that while girls and boys are just as likely to own the same kinds of devices, they use them in slightly different ways and in different frequencies (e.g., girls and older teens send more texts). Also, age seems to play a part as well, with younger teens 12-13 being at the fulcrum of device attainment and online participation. Thus, social technology use continues to become increasingly important—especially to determine the kinds of communication that are happening through the different types of social technology.

Social Technology and Peer Interaction

The previous section established that many teenagers are using social technology tools and the introduction to the study focused on the connection between virtual networks and face-to-face environments.

Teenagers use multiple social technology tools to connect with one another and access information. Further, they tend to connect with those they already know, and many of these peer connections can be found by way of their school-based networks. This section considers teen motivation for technology usage and the impact of that technology. Issues such as benefits and harms of technology utilization will be addressed.

Social Technology Potential Benefits and Motivators for Youth Use

Understanding foundational information about these tools is one thing, but digging deep into what these tools really are is another issue. Therefore, it is important to explore what motivates individuals to use these tools and what benefits they receive from taking part in them. This section will focus on the extension of peer culture, pushing teens online due to restricting public space, and building technology skills.

Humans are societal beings and generally have a strong desire to belong to and be part of a group (boyd, 2008; Coyle & Vaughn, 2008). The most obvious benefit to participating in virtual networks is that individuals have the opportunity to interact with their friends and share what has been happening with them when there is a physical space between them (boyd, 2008; Juvonen & Gross, 2008; Subrahmanyam & Greenfield, 2008). Social technology never closes—you can always pick up your phone, open your tablet, or boot up your computer to log into a social network site or instant messenger. Thus, these environments provide a space where individuals can access peer networks at any time of the day to gossip, support, collaborate, share information, flirt or joke in a way that extends, nurtures, and maintains friendships, as well as interests (Ito et al., 2008; Ito et al., 2010; Williams & Merten, 2008). These sites also allow youth to keep each other company when physically isolated from one another, and to share cultural tidbits from the day (boyd, 2007c).

The aforementioned connections to youth peer networks are especially important as teenagers clash with their parents to assert their independence and work to establish peer social hierarchy (Varjas, Henrich, & Meyers, 2009). They also provide a space where individuals can support one another through difficult times, talk through problems to find solutions, or just "vent." Research has shown social network sites to help teens to ease tensions (Ito et al., 2010) and even work through the death of a peer by enabling users to grieve by leaving messages for the deceased (Williams & Merten, 2009). Social network sites also provide those who struggle socially a chance to make connections (Jackson, 2006). Individuals who are either socially awkward or find trouble in expressing themselves verbally get the chance to show people who they are through written text which they can think through and modify before posting.

These spaces become a safe place for individuals to "play" and to negotiate their identity (Ito et al., 2010). This is especially important for teenagers who are struggling to figure out who they are and who they want to be. Social technology tools provide individuals the opportunity to create a profile space and identity that expresses their self-image (boyd, 2007a). Individuals take pictures and compose messages on their cell phones and laptop computers and thereby express themselves. Further, on social network sites they sift through pictures, decide what to write about themselves in the "about me" section, and identify favorite books and music interests that represent how they want to appear to their peer network. Thus, they negotiate presentations of self while keeping in mind their connections with others in their peer network (boyd & Ellison, 2007) and comments others post about their site aspects (Williams & Merten, 2008).

Social network profiles are important in that they represent a virtual proxy for self-identity (boyd, 2007b). People tend to put their "best" images forward according to how they might be perceived (boyd, 2008) and hide those things they might be interested in that do not make them look the way they might want to appear to their various networks.

While working on their identities, teenagers also learn what is socially acceptable within their peer group by engaging in the social network world by looking at friends' and friends of friends' profiles which is considered to be a form of entertainment that passes the time (boyd, 2007b). Through such activities teenagers compare identities (Barker, 2009), which is a socialization process at work as it reflects the physical, face-to-face school culture. As with this culture, social network environments teach individuals self-control (i.e., what to post/what not to post), tolerance (i.e., accepting others' posts), and respect for one another. This environment also allows them the opportunity to view multiple perspectives on things, and to learn how to express themselves in a healthy manner (Hinduja & Patchin, 2009).

Further, learning how to interact appropriately with others in their peer groups is an "important part of the social and cultural practices and habitus" (North et al., 2008, p. 907). This means that it is really all about friends, who you know, everyday life, and where you "hang out" (boyd, 2007b; boyd, 2007d). If a good number of a person's friends were not present on the site, they would be less likely to be involved. Since 2006, taking part in sites such as these is "essential to being *cool* at school" because that is where everyone is (boyd, 2007b, p. 1). In a very short time these sites have become essential aspects of students' social lives (Strom & Strom, 2005).

A further motivator for teenagers to use these kinds of sites is that it makes them feel good. Lenhart et al. (2011), in *Teens, Kindness, and Cruelty on Social Network Sites*, found that "65% of social media using teens have had an experience on a social network site that made them feel good about themselves" (p. 4). Furthermore, 58% of these teens "have felt closer to another person because of an experience on a social network site" (p. 4). Therefore, we see teenagers feeling good about themselves and feeling closer to others due to interaction on these sites—two very important aspects of growing up and navigating the world between childhood and adulthood.

While social technology provides teens the ability to extend their peer relationships, the opportunity to develop their identity and to feel good about yourself, physical location can also be a motivator for social technology use among teens as there is a lack of space, created by us as a society, for teens to physically occupy.

Another reason that teen social technology use has grown in popularity is that they provide a population that is typically limited in mobility, due to being unable to drive and needing to observe parental restrictions, a space to hangout (boyd, 2007a). An eternal struggle for teenagers often resides in finding physical locations outside of school where they can connect socially. One aspect of this problem is the suburbanization of America, which has created physical distances between teenagers while simultaneously constructing barriers to physical social connection (boyd, 2007a; Ito et al., 2010). However, even if teens can get rides from their parents or have their own transportation to places such as the mall, restaurants, or other public establishments, they are often not welcomed there. For example, malls may impose rules that limit those 17 and younger to only entering the mall after 3 p.m. on Fridays and Saturdays with a chaperone that is over

21 (Kirchen, 2008). Policies such as this, while beneficial for businesses, severely limit the number and ways teenagers interact with one another and tend to push them towards texting, talking to one another on the phone, and frequenting social network sites.

Some students have highly regulated schedules full of activities and homework, while others have parents who fear for their children's safety and react by limiting the amount of time they are allowed to leave the house (boyd, 2007b). Factors such as these limit face-to-face interaction opportunities outside of school grounds. Further, social technology tools also provide spaces for youth that are private from parent view, much like their bedroom culture (boyd, 2007c; boyd, 2008). Like bedrooms, they have the ability to allow entry to outsiders—except in the case of parental force—and to decorate it the way they please. While things such as social network sites are private in that you have the option to allow only those you add to see your information, they are public in the respect that those that you add have free access to your information. However, their social technology communicative platforms become one of the few spaces—besides their private bedrooms—that teens can control.

Potential Harms When Engaging in Social Technology Use

Many things that were cited as benefits and motivators to using the social network sites can potentially be used in harmful ways as well. Potential harms of social technology use by young people generally emit images of being contacted by strangers, computer viruses, hacking, pedophilic attempts, e-advertising, sexual intimidation, pornographic websites, unwanted webcams, cost, technical failure, and looking at other inappropriate sites (Vandebosch & Van Cleemput, 2008). While all these are valid concerns, this section will examine additional problematic sides to the use of social technology, identity creation, having 24-hour a day, 7-day a week access to peer networks, and using technological skills for unsupportive means.

Another large issue and potential harm with participation in the tools that social technology perpetuates is that in many circumstances it revolves around creating one's identity to be something true to themselves, and for it to be displayed for others to see. It is also necessary to look at media culture that heavily influences society and could contribute to how open teens have become with their information. Reality television has quickly become a cultural staple of and shapes the way people view themselves. Primetime sitcoms and dramas are disappearing while reality television programs such as "Survivor," "The Jersey Shore," "Teen Mom," "The Voice," "The Real Word/Road Rules Challenge," "American Idol," "Dancing with the Stars," "The Biggest Loser," "The Bachelorette," and "The Real Housewives" thrive. In these shows "regular" people are the stars, and they share their life story with the audience. It can be argued that reality programming has changed the way many people see things and has altered what is appropriate to share; this can be seen in the overabundance of personal information shared on the web via message boards, video sharing sites, and social network sites (Hinduja & Patchin, 2009, p. 81).

When individuals put themselves on display for others they do not always display their true thoughts, rather venturing towards what might be acceptable for those reading the profile to accept and find "normal." Trying to fit into peer culture is hard enough, but when different forms of power are thrown into the situation it gets pretty tricky. For example, imagine that you are a 14 year old trying to gain the constant acceptance of your peers and your mother requests to be your Facebook "friend." It is socially awkward to ignore or reject those that have power over you—whether it is a parent, a family member, a future employer, or a college admission board (boyd, 2007a). There are many things kids do that they do not want their parents to see. There may be adverse consequences to posting pictures of participating in risky behaviors (e.g., drinking, using drugs, holding firearms, etc.) as potential employers, prospective colleges and universities, parents, and other persons may find them.

Some individuals circumvent this risk by creating multiple profiles—one that caters to their peer group and one that is acceptable by adult/professional standards (Subrahmanyam & Greenfield, 2008). However, if friends become friends with people in power (e.g., parents or teachers) you can easily be found on their friend list and your "double profile life" can be ended quickly. While the splintering of one's identity and bending towards the norms of a peer network are troubling, it is also important to speak to how the constant access can lead to conflicts and unsupportive behavior, such as cyberbullying.

While teens may be drawn to social network sites to build peer connections and further construct self-esteem, they also report negative outcomes as well. Lenhart et al. (2011), in *Teens, Kindness, and Cruelty on Social Network Sites*, indicate that participation in social network sites can result in face-to-face confrontations, the ending of friendships, problems with parents, and anxiety about going to school. Table 3 illustrates the bad experiences that teens reported from using social network sites.

Table 3: *Bad Experiences Using Social Network Sites*

Experience	Reporting Experience (%)
Resulted in face-to-face confrontation	25%
Ended their friendship with someone	22%
Caused a problem with their parents	13%
Felt nervous about going to school	13%
Participated in a physical fight	8%
Gotten into trouble at school	6%

This data illustrates the connection between social technology and out-of-school communication showing that engaging with peers in social network environments can, in some circumstances, lead to face-to-face confrontations, friendships ending, anxiety around going to school, and physical fights.

While there are many potential benefits for teens participating in virtual peer-networked environments, these spaces can also be used to extend bullying from the "playground" to an always-on, 24-hour a day, 7-day a week space. This space, as documented earlier, can be a great benefit for teenagers struggling to become an independent being and negotiate the social hierarchy of their schooling experience because they have access to their supportive peer networks all the time. However, networks are not always supportive.

Many of the things that were cited as potential benefits can be seen as potential harms with regard to the social technology peer network space. While it is easy to positively communicate and interact with your friends, it is quick and just as easy to spread rumors, inflict fear, create a sense of helplessness, instill humiliation, and socially sabotage peers (Hinduja & Patchin, 2009; Mason, 2008; Strom & Strom, 2005). Hinduja and Patchin (2009) indicate that technology-savvy participants can cyberbully their peers in these popular ways:

- By taking the information that the victim posts on their social network profile while negotiating their identity to make a fake site, altering their information in a humiliating manner and sharing with members of the peer network.
- By stealing—or by being given in an act of intimacy (e.g., being "best friends" or in a romantic relationship)—passwords, logging into an individuals' account, changing their profile in an embarrassing way, and/or sending mean and inappropriate messages to those on that person's list of friends.
- By sending or posting messages that are threatening, mean, rude, or inappropriate to the cell phone or social network sites of the victim
- By sending or posting messages degrading the victim on other wall message areas or cell phones of people in the peer network that might support and add to the bullying as they fully understand that the victim can only delete messages on their own wall or cell phone.

Social technology tools create large audiences as teens tend to have hundreds of friends in their peer networks and information that can damage one's reputation can be spread to all of these individuals instantaneously, and it can not be retrieved (Juvonen & Gross, 2008; Strom & Strom, 2005; Willard, 2006). Wolak, Mitchell, and Finkelhor (2007) surveyed individuals 10-17 (n=1,500) in 2005 and found that 59% of incidents by known peers involved messages posted or sent for others to see. Since technology can quickly spread information to a large audience with a constant presence, it can leave victimized teenagers with a feeling that there is no escape. Having the feeling that there is no escape can lead to school violence, participation in risky behaviors, and even suicide (Hinduja & Patchin, 2009).

As with the quick and easy access to friends, the 24-hour a day, 7-day a week constant access can be particularly problematic for those who are victims of cyberbullying. In traditional school bullying the individuals could leave the schoolyard or cafeteria to head home to a place of safety (Jackson, 2006). Social networks provide connections, which can provide emotional support but can also produce connections with negative influences. With these technologies, cyberbullies can harass their victims after school and all day on the weekends and school holidays, leaving no escape for those that are victims—they can even be victimized when they are not online (Frederick, 2009; Hinduja & Patchin, 2009; Jackson, 2006; Stover, 2006; Wagner, 2008; Wolfsberg, 2006). Teens may feel that they can not escape cyberbullying, which is exacerbated by feelings of helplessness in not being able to do anything about it. They do not like to tell adult figures in fear of losing access to this integral network.

Another issue with cyberbullying with social technology tools is the feeling of being anonymous and detached due to the physical space between individuals. Individuals may be freed from the constraints of appropriate behavior, not think about the consequences, and say things they normally would not say in a face-to-face setting (Hinduja & Patchin, 2009). Not actually seeing how their words affect the person for whom they were meant, cyberbullies are less likely to feel regret, sympathy, or compassion for their victims (Strom & Strom, 2005; Wolfsberg, 2006). Researchers also believe that the lack of parental supervision facilitates cyberbullying as many parents do not understand or have social network profiles, which means they are not likely to view their children's profiles for assessing their appropriateness (Rosen, Cheever, & Carrier, 2008; Subrahmanyam & Greenfield, 2008).

Summary: Social Technology and Peer Interaction—Benefits and Harms

Social technology use has many benefits to participation and often affects youth in a positive manner. Not only does it allow for the isolation in the after-school space to be decreased, it creates a space where youth can connect to extend the peer culture network to give support to one another, negotiate their identity, and learn norms of participating in that particular peer network. Further, social technology provides an important space to youth that lack mobility due to not having a car or driver's license, as well as being shut out of popular venues such as shopping malls. In the end it also provides them with a private space that they can both make and call their own. However, this private space does not always provide a positive experience as it allows for the further reproduction of stratification and creates issues regarding multiple audiences. Furthermore, the constant and consistent access to social technology tools gives a 24-hour a day, 7-day a week access which can be especially troubling when individuals are bullied.

In order to study the cyberbullying phenomenon in depth, foundational bullying literature must be reviewed first.

BULLYING

While the focus of this study is cyberbullying, it is also prudent to review briefly the literature regarding traditional bullying. Traditional bullying has been studied in a limited fashion in the United States for the past few decades, and more prominently even longer throughout the world. This section will first discuss what bullying is before looking at victim characteristics, bullying characteristics, and where bullying tends to take place.

What is Bullying?

While bullying can happen in many places, it often occurs where the individuals affected can not escape—like schools (Smith et al., 1999). Bullying is difficult to define. Many times researchers struggle with whether a behavior is bullying or is just teasing (Harris & Petrie, 2003). Olweus (1993) distinguishes between the two by indicating that "a student is being bullied or victimized when he or she is exposed, repeatedly and over time, to negative actions on the part of one or more other students" (p. 9). Olweus goes on to describe negative actions as being repeatedly intentionally inflicted in varying (i.e., verbal, physical, or other as in exclusion) nature. Bullying does not occur when both students are at the same strength—physically, psychologically, or socially—as a key feature of bullying is the bully taking advantage of the victim's helplessness (Olweus, 1993; Sampson, 2009).

Bullying incidence and physical elements of bullying, tend to decline with age (Harris & Petrie, 2003; Nansel, et al., 2001; Olweus, 1993; Seals & Young, 2003). Bullying is usually perpetrated by those in the same grade level (Sampson, 2009; U.S. Department of Health and Human Services, 2003). Further, boys are exposed to more direct forms of bullying than girls, who are exposed to more indirect forms of bullying (Olweus, 1993; Sampson, 2009; U.S. Department of Health and Human Services, 2003). Direct forms of bullying are considered to be things like taunting, threatening gestures, hitting, using a weapon while indirect forms include influencing others to commit direct forms of bullying, spreading rumors, ignoring others intentionally, and excluding others on purpose (Harris & Petrie, 2003).

Seals and Young (2003) found that boys were more likely to be bullies and females were more likely to be bully victims, while Nansel et al. (2001) found that boys were more likely to be both perpetrators and victims. These findings, like much of the bullying findings, do not corroborate one another and differences could be attributed to the way bullying was defined and the kinds of bullying (i.e., physical, verbal, relational) that were measured which were not described. Bullying findings also show that class size and whether a child lives and attends school in an urban or rural area have no to very little impact on bullying frequency (Olweus, 1993; Seals & Young, 2003). Different forms of bullying can happen anywhere and are not necessarily associated with a specific gender, class size, or area.

Victim Characteristics

Victims can have many different characteristics that make them ideal targets for bullying. Victims of bullying tend to be anxious (American Medical Association, 2002; Harris & Petrie, 2003; Olweus, 1978; Olweus, 1993; Sampson, 2009; Wolpert, 2005) and insecure (Olweus, 1978; Olweus, 1993) with low self-esteem (American Medical Association, 2002; Harris & Petrie, 2003; Olweus, 1993), a negative self view (Olweus, 1993), and relatively few friends (Harris & Petrie, 2003; Olweus, 1978).

Bullying victimization has social, psychological, and physical impacts. Bullying can leave victims feeling socially isolated when at school (Harris & Petrie, 2003), which often leads to not speaking up in class (Olweus, 1978) and increased absenteeism (Wolpert, 2005; Harris & Petrie, 2003). This can lead to difficulty completing schoolwork (American Medical Association, 2002) and eventually dropping out of school (Harris & Petrie, 2003). Isolation and poor peer connections can leave bullying victims with psychological problems such as depression (American Medical Association, 2002; Harris & Petrie, 2003; Sampson, 2009) and prolonged self-esteem issues (American Medical Association, 2002), as well as increased physical ailments such as colds and migraine headaches (American Medical Association, 2002; Wolpert, 2005). These feelings of isolation from their peer group and accompanying problems have the potential to foment suicidal ideation

(American Medical Association, 2002) and completion of suicide attempts (Harris & Petrie, 2003; Sampson, 2009).

Bully Characteristics

Unfortunately, bullies do not fully comprehend how much their bullying bothers their victims due to a lack of empathy (Harris & Petrie, 2003; Olweus, 1993; Sampson, 2009). Compared to victims, bullies have average popularity (Sampson, 2009) and are more likely to feel secure, less afraid, and less anxious in school than their victim counterpart (Olweus, 1978). Bullies tend to be impulsive (American Medical Association, 2002; Olweus, 1993), have dominant personality traits (American Medical Association, 2002; Sampson, 2009), have difficulty following rules (American Medical Association, 2002; Harris & Petrie, 2003), have positive views of violence (Olweus, 1993; American Medical Association, 2002), and generally have more overall aggression—towards students and adults alike (e.g., teachers, family members, etc.). (Olweus, 1993; Harris & Petrie, 2003; Sampson, 2009). Some researchers attribute these adverse characteristics to poor relationships with parental figures. For example, Olweus (1978) indicates that these characteristics could be a result of children having less strong and less positive relationships to their parents. The American Medical Association (2002) goes into more depth indicating parental actions such as lack of warmth, lack of involvement, lack of supervision, and a harsh form of discipline that could potentially influence bullying behavior.

A shared understanding currently exists among researchers that bullying victims are prone to depression, and to having poor academic performance due to a decreased attendance to avoid bullying. However, researchers have also studied the overarching and longer-term impacts of being a bully. Dake, Price, and Telljohann (2003) found that bullies were significantly more likely to become involved in self-destructive behaviors such as alcohol use, tobacco use, and fighting (Dake, Price, and Telljohann, 2003). Further, they found significant relationships with weapon-carrying, cheating on tests, stealing, vandalism, trouble with police, and skipping school (Dake, Price, & Telljohann, 2003). Like these findings, the American Medical Association (2002) found that there was an increase for bullies in delinquent/antisocial behaviors (e.g., vandalism, shoplifting, truancy, drug use), which continued into young adulthood. Further, they were more apt to drink, smoke, and have bad school performance, with one in four boy bullies having a criminal record by 30 (American Medical Association, 2002).

Due to having a dominant personality, partaking in risk-taking behaviors (e.g., weapon-carrying, drug use, alcohol use, etc.), and having aggression towards teachers and students bullies, like victims, are more likely to drop out of school than the average student (Harris & Petrie, 2003). With no positive interventions to change behavior, childhood and teenage bullies have the potential to become adult bullies (Sampson, 2009). Harris and Petrie (2003) also found that bullies were more likely to treat their wife and children more aggressively which they concluded was only perpetuating the bullying cycle by creating children who would also bully others.

Where Does Bullying Occur?

Many individuals assume that a lot of bullying is done before and after school. While some bullying is done during this time, it is also important to acknowledge the bullying most often takes place at school in unsupervised spaces such as classrooms when the teacher walks out for a moment, playgrounds, hallways, restrooms, and lunchrooms (Harris & Petrie, 2003; Sampson, 2009). The U.S. Department of Health and Human Services (2003) reported that between 40% and 75% of bullying takes place during these breaks where many unsupervised spaces are accessible by students. Seals and Young (2003) surveyed students to find that of those that had experience with bullying, 79.3% were bullied in class, 79.7% during lunch and recess, 35.2% on their way to school, and 63.9% on their way home. Harris and Petrie (2003) surveyed both middle and high school students to determine where bullying was most likely to take place, and to see if there was a difference between the two age sets. Findings regarding where bullying takes place by middle and high school are reported in Table 4.

Middle and high school results are similar for being bullied during unsupervised spaces within the school day like during class and lunch, as well as at after-school events. In middle school, the recess period is another popular time for bullying to take place; in high school class breaks offer another venue sometimes utilized. Results from both middle and high school reflect a relatively low amount of bullying taking place before school, with a higher amount taking place after school. This pattern could be attributed to bullies being uncertain where their victims originate (i.e., where they live, getting access to them during their to-school route, etc.), and having an understanding of how to access victims during the end of the school day period.

Table 4: ***Where Bullying Takes Place***

Place	Middle School	High School
During Class	77%	78%
During Lunch	83%	75%
During School Events	63%	66%
Recess	61%	NR
Class Breaks	NR	46%
On the Way to School	34%	27%
On the Way Home from School	62%	57%

Summary: Bullying, Victimization, and Spaces

While bullying behavior is often difficult to define, it incorporates three major components that include: an intent to harm, a power differential, and a series of repeated actions. Bullying affects both the victim and the bully in adverse ways. The victim tends to be anxious and insecure with low self-esteem and few friends, characteristics which can draw attention from a more dominant bullying individual. Bullying victimization creates uneasiness within victims that often increases school absenteeism. Missing school further facilitates the isolation of the victim and the loss of peer connections; these individuals are subsequently more likely to drop out of school than the average student. This isolation can have a debilitating effect on victims as it has the potential to produce feelings of depression and suicidal ideation. Conversely, bullies are more secure and less anxious than victims, with a positive view of violence and the benefits of overall aggressive behavior. These traits lead the way for bullies being more likely to carry weapons, experiencing trouble in school and with authorities, as well as being more likely to become an adult bully in the home and/or workplace. This information is important to incorporate into future studies regarding the impact of new mediums—such as social technology—on bullying. Further, bullying literature shows that it tends to take place in unsupervised spaces during breaks in the school day (between class periods, within-class breaks, recess, lunch, etc.) and during after-school events; these spaces may be likened to the unsupervised spaces provided by social technology.

CYBERBULLYING

There are few empirical cyberbullying studies focusing on middle and high school students in the United States (Agatston, Kowalski, & Limber, 2007; Allen, 2012; Hinduja & Patchin, 2007; Hinduja & Patchin, 2008; Hinduja & Patchin, 2010a; Hinduja & Patchin, 2010b; Hinduja & Patchin, 2013; Kowalski, Morgan, & Limber, 2012; Mishna, Saini, & Solomon, 2009; Patchin & Hinduja, 2006; Raskauskas & Stoltz, 2007; Sengupta & Chaudhuri , 2011; Vandebosch & Van Cleemput, 2008; Varjas, Henrich, & Meyers, 2009; Williams & Guerra, 2007); those highlighting the use of the inclusivity of social technology tools (i.e., cell phones and social network sites) are even fewer—and virtually non-existent in a mixed methods analytical approach. In this section cyberbullying conceptualization will be discussed before reviewing extant studies.

Conceptualizing Cyberbullying

Those researchers who have explored the cyberbullying phenomenon thus far do not seem to operate on the same basic definitions, which makes findings difficult to compare. Some researchers broadly describe cyberbullying by defining it as bullying via an electronic medium (Li, 2006; Patchin & Hinduja, 2006). Cyberbullying is much more complex as the definition does not differentiate between the different kinds of electronic mediums. Different forms of technology can promote very different kinds of anonymity in cyberbullying. For example, instant messaging and email can be manipulated by cyberbullies who anonymously create fake screen names or email addresses to threaten or make fun of peers. Social network cyberbullies, conversely, are typically less anonymous (even though many teenagers do add individuals they do not know) as they have to accept a person as their "friend" and give permission to those that want to view their information and comment on their pages. Cyberbullying by this method can easily start in cyberspace but manifests itself in actual face-to-face environments such as schools with a known presence. Some authors have employed traditional bullying definitions to clarify cyberbullying definitions.

Many of the reviewed studies used a basis of traditional bullying to create their definitions. However, traditional bullying also seems to suffer from conceptualization issues, as there are many different versions of definitions utilized by published researchers. Many refer to Olweus, a major leader in the bullying field, as defining the act of bullying in terms of the combination of three major components—namely, power differential, intent to inflict harm, and repetition (as cited in Patchin & Hinduja, 2006; Vandebosch & Van Cleemput, 2008; Varjas et al., 2009). Even though these components were made for the study of traditional bullying, these elements of harassment settings can be transferred to the cyberbullying field.

In the case of cyberbullying these three components are apparent, but they are often difficult to decipher and apply towards real world definitions and the conceptualization around cyberbullying. The intent to harm in cyberbullying focuses on the intent to be hurtful and hinges on victim impact, which itself revolves around perception (Vandebosch & Van Cleemput, 2008). In cyberbullying there is also a power differential. While bullying is often housed in the physical or social realms, the power differential in cyberbullying often makes itself apparent through the power of understanding how to use and navigate the intricacies of the several different social technologies. These social technologies can be utilized to either become veiled in anonymity or disseminate information quickly (Dooley, Pyzalski, & Cross, 2009; Vandebosch & Van Cleemput). In cyberbullying, the component of repetition is somewhat ambiguous. Repetitiveness is typically defined as happening more than once. However, in cyberbullying one action by a cyberbully can be spread to hundreds of people (e.g., by an embarrassing picture text or Facebook post) at once which, to the victim is repetitive and has major impact as many people get the information and have potential to contribute to the cyberbullying action (Dooley, Pyzalski, & Cross, 2009).

Studies in the field often use some or all of the Olweus components in their definitions of cyberbullying. Hinduja and Patchin (2006) define cyberbullying as a "willful and repeated harm inflicted through an electronic medium" (p. 152). This definition mentions harm through an electronic medium, but fails to detail what that might mean and who is doing the bullying—individuals or groups. Further, it does include the concepts of being intentional and repeated, but does not include power differential, which is an important aspect of Olweus' definition and is apparent in social technology cyberbullying in that individuals have power over one another to share unwanted information or spread rumors quickly to many others instantaneously.

Agatston, Kowalkski, and Limber (2007) define cyberbullying as "using the Internet or other digital technologies such as cellular phones and personal digital assistants to be intentionally mean or harass others" (p. S60). The asset of this definition is that it gives some detail regarding what is meant by "electronic medium." While it includes Olweus' aspect of intention, it fails to mention the need for the action to be repeated (which can be seen in cyberbullying either by the repeated action or the pervasive reading) or power included in the act. Further, it does not make it clear whether individuals or groups are performing the actions.

Dooley, Pyzalski, and Cross (2009) cite the definition found in Smith et al. (2008) in that cyberbullying is "an aggressive, intentional act carried out by a group or an individual, using electronic forms of contact, repeatedly and over time against a victim who cannot easily defend him or herself" (p. 182). This definition not only includes Olweus' three components of bullying, but also indicates that it can be carried out by either an individual or a group. However, this particular definition does not include specificity regarding electronic forms of contact. Literature shows that it is important to define cyberbullying by including Olweus' three components, describing who is doing the bullying action, and by using which forms of electronic means.

Another set of conceptualization issues comes not in the essential components involved, but rather in the kinds of bullying behavior that actually exist. Some studies cite the confusion between there being two forms (indirect vs. direct bullying), three forms (verbal, physical, and social/relational), and four forms (teasing/taunting, physical aggression, verbal aggression, and submissive/passive) of bullying (Mason, 2008; Varjas et al., 2009). In describing cyberbullying, even Hinduja and Patchin (2007) throw major and minor into the mix. McGuiness (2007) proposes there be four categories that utilize verbal, relational, physical, and cyberbullying. Further, Li (2008) defines cyberbullying by a constant comparison between it and bullying. This comparison is shown in Table 5.

Table 5: *Bullying and Cyberbullying Comparison*

Bullying	Cyberbullying
Direct/Visible	Anonymous
Specific Time/Place	Anytime
Slow Moving/Narrow Scope	Fast/Broad
Hard to Preserve	Easy to Preserve
Poor Teacher Relationships	Good Teacher Relationships
School Property	Off School Property

Li makes it clear that there are many integral differences between bullying and cyberbullying. However, Li makes many assumptions about cyberbullying in that it has to be anonymous even though that is not always the case. More importantly it is necessary to understand that not being physically face-to-face with one another does not always mean anonymity. In some kinds of cyberbullying there is anonymity (like emailing, instant messaging, or even creating a fake profile on a social network site), but in social network cyberbullying people typically add those they know. While cyberbullying can take place off of school grounds, it can also easily take place on school property in the school's computer lab or by students utilizing their mobile phones. A key feature of cyberbullying includes the aspect that makes social technology so appealing to its users because spaces are always available and cyberbullying can happen anywhere and everywhere (Mishna, Saini, & Solomon, 2009).

Current cyberbullying behavior researchers have made conceptualization choices in their studies that have advanced this nascent field of study. However, their definitions have been varied which makes it difficult to compare studies and find definitive answers within the cyberbullying phenomenon. In order to move the field forward a more common definition must be established. This study will define cyberbullying much like Dooley, Pyzalski, and Cross (2009) who used Smith et al.'s (2008) definition in that cyberbullying is "an aggressive, intentional act carried out by a group or an individual, using electronic forms of contact, repeatedly and over time against a victim who cannot easily defend him or herself" (p. 182). However, as discussed previously it is important to give some definition to the broad "electronic forms of contact" by listing some of the tools of social technology. Thus, this study will define cyberbullying as an aggressive, intentional act carried out by a group or an individual, using electronic forms of contact found by way of cell phones, computers, and portable devices (e.g., gaming, iPods, etc.), repeatedly and over time against a victim who cannot easily defend him or herself.

Current Studies

In this section available studies will be examined pertaining to perpetration and victimization, race and gender, age and use of the Internet, the relationship between being a bully and a cyberbully, and the relationship between cyberbullying and offline risky behaviors.

Patchin and Hinduja (2006) studied the cyberbullying phenomenon and found that 30% of those surveyed were victims, 11% bully others, and 47% witnessed an act of cyberbullying. The researchers operationalized cyberbullying as being ignored, disrespected, called names, threatened, picked on, made fun of, or had rumors spread about them. Their survey methodology focused on surveying the frequency of electronic bullying by gathering participants from visitors of a website for a popular music artist. While the researchers indicated that this musician was liked by the target population, they failed to take into account differences in the target population. Music tastes have the potential to be shaped by a differential in race and social class. Even though the survey turned out to be more of a convenience sample and not generalizable, it still provides reasonable grounds for starting to think about frequency and prevalence. In later work Hinduja and Patchin (2010b), as reported on their website (cyberbullying.us), surveyed a random sample of youth (n=4,441) aged 10-18 from one large school district in the southern United States and found 20.8% reported being cyberbullied over the course of their life with 7.5% reporting being victimized by cyberbullying over the past 30 days. Associated with this, but not necessarily thought of as cyberbullying, 14.3% of students reported being the victims of mean or hurtful comments online and 13.3% indicated they were the target of rumors online over the past 30 days. Nearly 20% of students reported that they had perpetrated a cyberbullying act over the course of their life with 8.6% indicated that they had cyberbullied others over the past 30 days. Some students (8.8%) revealed that, over the past 30 days, they had posted mean or hurtful comments about someone online and 6.8%

indicated that they had spread rumors about someone online, through text messages, or emails.

Juvonen and Gross (2008) found that 72% of respondents reported at least one online incident of bullying, but they did not identify how the survey items were operationalized. This percentage is much higher than what Hinduja and Patchin (2006) found. This could be due to operationalization, which was not revealed, or indicating to survey participants that one incident counted as bullying behavior. Kowalski and Limber (2007) gathered information from an adapted Olweus Bully/Victim Questionnaire (n=3767) and found that 11% had been electronically bullied in the last few months and 4% had bullied others while Li (2007) found that 14.5% of respondents were cyberbullies and that 24.9% were cyberbully victims. These two studies are much closer to the findings reported by Patchin and Hinduja (2006). Further, Li (2007) measured how many times victims had been victimized with the majority (59.1%) being victimized 1-3 times, 18.2% 4-10 times, and 22.7% over 10 times. However, Li's research is based on samples from Canada and China which seem to look like those in the U.S. but would need more research in order to confirm this assumption. Cyberbullying is indeed happening on a major scale, and further research is clearly needed that collects perpetration and victimization data, and which articulates the conceptualization and the variable operationalization process in proper depth.

Bullying literature shows that boys were more likely to be bullies and victims, with boys leaning more towards direct forms of bullying such as hitting while girls were more likely to take part in indirect bullying such as spreading rumors and promoting social exclusion. Dowell, Burgess, and Cavanaugh (2009) found, by way of an adapted Youth Internet Safety Survey conducted at one public and one parochial middle school in middle and upper-middle class areas (n=404), that girls spent significantly more time on the Internet during a typical week, had significantly more email addresses, and used instant messaging significantly more than did boys in those schools.

Hinduja and Patchin (2009) and Williams and Guerra (2007) found that there were no significant differences in offending or victimization by gender or race, while Li (2007) found that women were more likely to be victims in the study (Li, 2006). Ybarra and Mitchell (2007) found that boys were three times more likely than girls to be frequent perpetrators of online harassment. Dempsey (2009) also found that females were more likely to be victims of relational and cyberbullying than males, who in turn were more likely to report overt victimization. In their later data, Hinduja and Patchin (2010b) found that female respondents were more likely to report being cyberbullied and committing cyberbullying acts over their lifetime. Further, over the past 30 days females reported being more likely to have hurtful comments posted about them online and spreading rumors online about others. With contradicting data regarding gender and few studies looking at race as a factor more research must be done to determine relationships that may exist with cyberbullying engagement.

Hinduja and Patchin (2007) found that age and cyberbullying were related to a statistically significant degree; older youth were engaged in more problem behaviors than their younger counterparts. This is interesting because Varjas et al. (2009) focus their survey study (n=427) on both bullying and cyberbullying among middle school students. Middle schoolers are more likely to take part in traditional bullying as older students grow out of it. Williams and Guerra (2007) surveyed students in grades 5, 8, and 11 (n=2,293) in Colorado and found that Internet bullying seemed to peak in middle school and declined in high school. More research must be done to understand whether cyberbullying follows the pattern of traditional bullying where students are more likely to take part in it as a middle school student or if, due to the nature of things such as social network environments, it houses high school relational gossip and verbal bullying.

Unlike traditional physical bullying, as frequency of online harassment increases age tends to increase (Ybarra & Mitchell, 2007) showing that perhaps older students are utilizing social technology for social types of cyberbullying. Hinduja and Patchin (2007, 2009) also found a relationship between computer proficiency and being a cyberbully or being cyberbullied. Therefore, teenagers that have a better grasp of how to use the different functions of social technology could use their knowledge to participate in cyberbullying behavior. Allen (2012) conducted a mixed method study exploring the affect of texting messaging on cyberbullying in a suburban US high school. Allen's (2012) findings indicate that texting contributes to conflict and "drama" which may contribute to bullying and cyberbullying behavior.

Besides access, proficiency of technology use is important to mention. Proficient computer users may spend more time online. Hinduja and Patchin (2007, 2009), Ybarra and Mitchell (2007), and

Smith et al. (2008) all have reported a connection between time spent online and being a cyberbully or being cyberbullied. Those that were more proficient in computer usage and spent more time online were more likely to be engaged in cyberbullying activity. Pieschl, Porsch, Kahl, and Klockenbusch (2013) conducted an experimental study in Germany around cyberbullying and found that cyberbullying by a popular individual was more distressing to victims than cyberbullying by an unpopular individual. However, it is important to note that this study was conducted in Germany and there are yet to be studies of this nature conducted here in the United States. However, Hinduja and Patchin (2013) did find that perceptions of peers behaving similarly (e.g., cyberbullying others) was a contributing factor for participation in cyberbullying activity. Therefore, age, use of social technology, popularity, and perceptions of others may all play roles in cyberbullying engagement and also need further research.

Some researchers have found relationships between being a traditional bully and being a cyberbully victim. In their 2007 and 2009 studies, Hinduja and Patchin found that there was a relationship between being a traditional bully and being a cyberbully and/or a cyberbully victim. They concluded that experience with traditional bullying increased the risk of being cyberbullied (Hinduja & Patchin, 2009). Li (2007) also found relationships reported between being a bully and a cyberbully in that almost 30% were both. Interestingly enough, Li also found a tie between being both a cyberbully and being a cyberbully victim, as mentioned by Jackson's report in 2006 and Beran and Li (2007), a finding which could be attributed to retaliation measures taken. More research is needed on whether individuals that bully traditionally are more likely to bully in cyberspace, and how exactly physical peer groups overlap virtually. More importantly, research must be done to see if there are further connections to being a cyberbully and a cyberbully victim such as in forms of retaliation.

One of the key concerns of researchers, school administrators, and the general public revolves around the impact that cyberbullying has on offline behaviors. Those studying traditional bullying have found that bullying victims tend to worry, dislike themselves, and be depressed—all characteristics which can make them want to stay home from school and may indirectly affect their health (Berthold & Hoover, 2000; Boynton-Jarrett, Ryan, & Wright, 2008). Both bullying and being victimized by bullying have adverse impacts on participation in risky behaviors, as both tend to be more likely to drink alcohol, smoke or chew tobacco, and take illegal substances (Berthold & Hoover, 2000; Boynton-Jarrett et al., 2008). Further, bullies and bully victims are likely to associate with peers who have had the same experiences and cope by taking part in these same risky behaviors (Rusby, Forrester, Biglan, & Metzler, 2005). However, Tharp-Taylor, Haviland, & D-Amico (2009) found that the relationship between the risky behaviors existed only with those that had experienced victimization. This is not to say that cyberbullying perpetrators are not affected by their cyberbullying engagement. Campbell, Slee, Spears, Butler, and Kift (2013) recently studied the perceptions of cyberbullies in Australia and found that cyberbullies did not believe their bullying was harsh or had impact on their victims. Further, cyberbullies reported higher levels of stress, depression, anxiety, and social difficulty than their non-bullying counterparts.

Cyberbullying produces increased feelings of social anxiety and lowered self-esteem, characteristics which can have large impacts on youth and how they interact with the world (Dempsey, Sulkowski, Nichols, & Storch, 2009; Juvonen & Gross, 2008; Mason, 2008; Willard, 2006). One of the ways this can affect students is in how safe they feel while they are at school. Varjas et al. (2009) found that those that were cyberbullied did not associate their being cyberbullied with decreased feelings of school safety. While this might have a lot to do with how this item is measured and it being broad in looking at all cyberbullying, it would be interesting to investigate if students that were cyberbullied by ways of social technology by someone they knew from school would report feeling less safe at school.

Another impact of the stress and pressure of being cyberbullied and being the cyberbully is associated with school difficulties in that antisocial behavior can hurt the school environment by affecting academic and social outcomes, causing emotional and psychological trauma, and potentially leading to school violence (Bailey, 2008; Hinduja & Patchin, 2007; Hinduja & Patchin, 2009; Mason, 2008). Researchers also report connections between being a cyberbully and/or a cyberbully victim and engaging in risky behaviors such as alcohol and cigarette use (Bailey, 2008; Hinduja & Patchin, 2007; Hinduja & Patchin, 2009; Patchin & Hinduja, 2006; Mason, 2008; McGuinness, 2007), but for the most part these relationships have not been linked to empirical data (except studies by Hinduja and Patchin) and need to be explored in a more in-depth fashion. More research on other risky behaviors such as smoking marijuana, using prescription drugs recreationally, and using hard drugs—as well as levels of these behaviors—is also needed.

Some dismissing cyberbullying as a problem wonder if it can really harm anyone absent a physical threat (Mishna, Saini, & Solomon, 2009). However, the problem is much more complex than simply turning off the computer or cell phone. To young people that are cyberbullied it is not seen as a joke, and they often do not know what to do or to whom to turn to because turning the phone or computer off would further isolate them from their peer group and telling their parents could create a circumstance where they would take access to social technology away (Agatston, Kowalski, & Limber, 2007).

It is important to recognize that cyberbullies and victims are more likely to become adults with unstable relationships with needs for mental health services (Strom & Strom, 2005). These individuals are also more likely to skip school, have low levels of school commitment factors which can lead to academic underachievement that can affect future educational and employment opportunities (Mason, 2008; Stover, 2006). All of these things can lead to the bringing of a weapon to school, engaging in school violence, and suicide attempts (Bailey, 2008; Mason, 2008; Stover, 2006; Willard, 2006). Hinduja and Patchin (2010a) analyzed survey data from middle school students (n=1,963) in one large school district in the U.S. and found that those who had experienced traditional bullying or cyberbullying as a perpetrator or victim were more likely to have suicidal thoughts or attempt suicide than those who were not involved in bullying or cyberbullying behavior. Further analysis showed that victimization had a stronger relationship with suicidal thoughts than perpetration. While suicidal thoughts are important to recognize, so is school safety. Juvonen and Gross (2008) surveyed teens 12-17 (n=1,454) regarding engagement in cyberbullying behavior and found that of those that had been victims of cyberbullying and 60% retaliated on school grounds, and 28% retaliated both online and at school.

Therefore, there is a warranted concern that off-campus behavior that can take place virtually can manifest itself in our nation's schools (Stover, 2006; Willard, 2008) as individuals are frequently targeted, more than once, by those they know (Ybarra & Mitchell, 2004). Ybarra, Diener-West, and Leaf (2007) also reported a connection between cyberbullying and bringing a weapon to school. In their survey (n=1,588) of 10-15 year olds they found that cyberbullied youth were eight times more likely than all other youth to report carrying a weapon to school. Interestingly enough, while being cyberbullied or being a cyberbully can affect an individual at the time of the event, there seems to be connections between the offline behaviors that are a result of being a cyberbully or a cyberbully victim that can affect them long after the particular instance is over.

As cyberbullying research is in its infancy, researchers must work to understand the phenomenon and work with school staff, law enforcement, and the community to better inform cyberbullying prevention and intervention strategies. Recently Hinduja and Patchin (2013) reported that middle and high school students were deterred from cyberbullying engagement by potential punishments from the adults in their lives. Unfortunately parents have grown up in a different, non-digital age and may not be "technically" equipped to understand the tools their children are using. Likewise, teachers may not feel equipped to deal with cyberbullying either. Bradshaw, Waasdorp, O'Brennan, & Gulemetova (2013) analyzed data from a sample of National Education Association members (n=5,064) and found that both education support professionals and teachers reporting wanting more training related to cyberbullying—especially related to sexual orientation, gender, and race.

Summary: Cyberbullying

Current cyberbullying studies, at times, have discrepancies between them due to conceptualization and operationalization issues in the field which often makes it difficult to compare studies. Further, there are wide ranges in observed victimization rates and inconsistent findings when it comes to gender, age, and general feelings of school safety. Only one study (Li, 2006) investigated race, which leaves much more room for study of the cyberbullying phenomenon. Also, while some data exist on how traditional bullying behavior affects victims and bullies, there is insufficient evidence regarding relationships between engaging in cyberbullying behavior (as a victim or bully), school safety and offline risky behaviors such as carrying a weapon to school and partaking in alcohol and illegal drug use. Thus, more study around perpetration, victimization, and prevention strategies is clearly warranted.

SUMMARIZING THE LITERATURE RELATED TO CYBERBULLYING

The study of cyberbullying is still in the early stages of development; extreme differences are seen when it comes to conceptualization and operationalization in prior studies. The field must move towards a common definition that is differentiated from bullying but still incorporates the needed components from that area while specifying who is doing the bullying (individuals and/or groups) and noting the electronic means utilized (since different media produce different types of bullying). The extant cyberbullying research has been inconsistent and narrow in scope. The few studies which have been conducted demonstrate a relationship to cyberbullying, and traditional, perpetration. Further, these studies have been inconclusive regarding demographic variables such as race, gender, and age and their relationships to cyberbullying. While some literature indicates traditional bullying affects young people who are engaging in cyberbullying activity, more studies are needed that speak to how cyberbullying affects these young. Further research on engagement in cyberbullying activities and mental health (e.g., depression, worry, anxiety), indulging in risky behaviors (e.g., tobacco use, alcohol use, illegal substances), and the impact on academics (feelings of school safety, skipping school, dropping out, etc.) is also necessary.

As technology becomes ubiquitous, cyberbullying and its variations (cell, instant messaging, social network, etc.) are emerging as a critical research topic. Solutions are not as simple as telling parents to forbid teenage participation in virtual networks or take social technologies away from their teenagers if cyberbullying becomes a problem. It can be quite dangerous to live in a world of simplistic labels because there are so many complexities in the world. An important "challenge for parents and schools alike is to eliminate the negative uses of electronic media while preserving their significant contributions to education and social connection" (Subrahmanyam & Greenfield, 2008, p. 120). Research is needed that provides us with a clear picture of how social technology benefits a teenager's development, how social technology and cyberbullying are associated with race, class, and gender, as well as how cyberbullying and victimization contribute to risky behaviors, academic underachievement, school violence, and personal well-being.

This study focuses on corroborating perpetration and victimization frequency, along with relationships to demographic variables and risky behaviors. This study also investigates what cyberbullying is to middle and high school students by collecting their perceptions through focus groups. During these focus groups students explained how they defined cyberbullying behavior, how cyberbullying affected their peer interactions, how cyberbullying affected their school environment, and what, if any, relationship existed between cyberbullying engagement and engaging in risky behaviors.

CHAPTER 3

About the Study

> Mixed methods research is an appropriate methodological choice if it is the most suitable way to answer the research questions of interest (Tashakkori & Teddlie, 2003) and when the qualitative or quantitative approach alone cannot adequately address the research problems to be addressed (Creswell, 2009).

For this study, an explanatory mixed methods approach was selected. As indicated in the previous sections of this book there is a significant deficit in the extant education, criminal justice, and public health literature that needs to address how cyberbullying extends to the school environment. In order to sufficiently study the cyberbullying phenomenon two major facets must be considered—the extension of peer networks and cyberbullying connections depicting incidence, characteristics, relationships, and impact. It was necessary for this study to examine how peer networks extend from the school day to social technology to school again. It was also necessary to focus on cyberbullying incidence, characteristics of victimization and perpetration, as well as impact featuring potential relationships with school violence, teenage suicide, and risky behaviors such as smoking cigarettes, drinking alcohol, and taking drugs. Engagement in these behaviors can effect schools and have consequences that follow children well past their schooling years. The following section will posits research questions addressing important aspects of the phenomenon.

RESEARCH QUESTIONS

Research questions should always be at the center of a study and should drive the study's major elements (i.e., study design, methodological choice, data collection questions, data analysis, etc.). The purpose of this explanatory mixed methods study was to utilize quantitative and qualitative data collection to examine cyberbullying that features social technology among middle and high school students guided by the following research questions:

Quantitative	1. How frequently do middle and high school students engage in cyberbullying behaviors?
	2. Which demographic variables (i.e., gender, age, race, etc.) describe cyberbullying activity for middle and high school students?
	3. How does social technology cyberbullying relate to risky behaviors and feelings of school safety for middle and high school students?
Qualitative (Central)	4. What is social technology cyberbullying for middle and high school students?
Qualitative (Sub questions)	4a. How do students define cyberbullying?
	4b. What experiences have they had with cyberbullying activity?
	4c. Where does cyberbullying take place?
	4d. How has cyberbullying impacted their peer interactions?
	4e. How has cyberbullying activity impacted their perceptions of their school environment?
	4f. How has cyberbullying activity impacted their participation in risky behaviors?
Mixed Methods	5. To what extent and in what ways do qualitative data collection (i.e., focus groups and open-ended survey questions) among middle and high school students serve to contribute to a more comprehensive understanding of social technology use and cyberbullying for middle and high school students?

Rationale for Quantitative Question Choices

Empirical cyberbullying studies are few in number (Agatston, Kowalski, & Limber, 2007; Allen, 2012; Hinduja & Patchin, 2007; Hinduja & Patchin, 2008; Mishna, Saini, & Solomon, 2009; Patchin & Hinduja, 2006; Hinduja & Patchin, 2010a; Hinduja & Patchin, 2010b; Hinduja & Patchin, 2013; Raskauskas & Stoltz, 2007; Vandebosch & Van Cleemput, 2008; Varjas, Henrich, & Meyers, 2009; Williams & Guerra, 2007). Those studies that do exist have presented inconclusive evidence regarding incidence, victimization, perpetration, and impact. A number of anecdotal essays have presented hints at potential relationships between cyberbullying, demographics, and impact behavior. Past research—and gaps in that research—have provided the basis for the quantitative research questions developed for this study.

The first question revolves around the frequency of cyberbullying activities. Patchin and Hinduja (2006) found that 11% of survey participants identified themselves as cyberbullies and 30% reported being victims of cyberbullying. However, Juvonen and Gross (2008) found that 72% of their survey participants were classified as cyberbully victims. Li (2007) documented that 14.5% of the participants identified themselves as cyberbullies, and concluded that 24.9% of her sample were *bona-fide* cyberbully victims. While Li's 2007 findings corroborate Patchin and Hinduja's perpetration and victimization findings, her study focused on survey participants in Canada and China. With a large discrepancy between the Patchin and Hinduja findings of victimization (30%) and those of Juvonen and Gross (72%) it is important to add to the frequency of perpetration and victimization data with research on the following question:

Research Question 1: How frequently do middle and high school students engage in cyberbullying behaviors?

While frequency of perpetration and victimization is important, it is also necessary to look at key demographic variables and how they might be related to cyberbullying activity. Cyberbullying and traditional bullying researchers have posited theory derived from the observation that since girls are more likely to partake in indirect bullying that features relational and verbal aspects, that gender would make a difference in cyberbullying activity. However, Hinduja and

Patchin (2009) found that there were no significant differences in either cyberbullying offending or victimization by gender. Further, Li (2007) and Dempsey et al. (2009) found that women were more likely to be victims of cyberbullying, but Li (2006) found that gender did not have a significant relationship in victimization in his study. While there seems to be little evidence that gender plays a significant role in contemporary cyberbullying activity, there is still not enough evidence to rule it out as a possibility.

Only one study that focused on cyberbullying has looked at the effect of race. Hinduja and Patchin (2009) found that there were no significant differences in either offending or victimization by race. It is important to not overlook race, and to dig deep into findings around race. For example, in the one study that has investigated race, why was it not shown to be a significant finding? Was it due to the sampling in choosing websites that might skew towards different races? Could it be an impact of the digital divide? Or could it be something else all together? Further, if race is found to be significant—why is it so? Is it more prevalent due to the target area being more of an urban area? Thus, it is important to incorporate race as a key research question. Therefore, it is important that these items serve as a basis for the following research question:

Research Question 2: Which demographic variables (i.e., gender, age, race, etc.) predict cyberbullying activity for middle and high school students?

One of the most important aspects of this study for researchers, law enforcement, and school personnel is to identify how cyberbullying activity affects teenage engagement in risky behaviors. Researchers report finding connections between being a cyberbully and/or a cyberbully victim and engaging in risky behaviors such as alcohol and cigarette use (Bailey, 2008; Hinduja & Patchin, 2007; Hinduja & Patchin, 2009; Patchin & Hinduja, 2006; Mason, 2008; McGuinness, 2007), but few have tested this connection through either quantitative or qualitative study. Research thus far has not examined relationships between cyberbullying and other risky behaviors such as marijuana, prescription, and hard drug use.

Varjas et al. (2009) found that students did not equate school safety to acts of cyberbullying. However, with social networks carrying over from physical spaces such as schools and into the online world via social technologies, there is a potential for problems to emerge in cyberspace and make themselves apparent in the physical—especially unsupervised—school space. With the lack of research looking at this aspect of social technologies it is important to focus on the following research question:

Research Question 3: How does social technology cyberbullying relate to risky behaviors and feelings of school safety for middle and high school students?

In combination these first three research questions provide a general picture of the cyberbullying phenomenon. They add to the existing literature when it comes to frequency, key demographics, risky behaviors, and feelings of school safety having relationships with cyberbullying engagement. This is a necessary component of the study as these areas in previous literature have been limited in the amount of study and generally inconclusive in their collective findings.

Research Question 4 (central qualitative question): What is social technology cyberbullying for middle and high school students?

This research question focuses on the central phenomenon of how social technology is used by middle and high school students to engage in cyberbullying activity, and explore what it means to them. It also paves the way for more detailed sub-questions with the first such question revolving around how cyberbullying is actually defined by teenagers. The research literature has defined cyberbullying in the past as requiring an electronic medium, specifying whether or not it is perpetrated by an individual or group, and by the three foundational features of bullying (repeated, intentional, and a power differential). Specifically, Vandebosch and Van Cleemput (2008) point out one of the largest issues regarding current research on cyberbullying in that there is a lack of conceptual clarity in regard to defining cyberbullying, a fact that leads to different operationalizations which measure different things. Further, they advocate for a clear definition for researchers, as well as a definition coinciding with research participant views. While the authors alluded to the need for a common definition and gathered information via focus groups regarding what cyberbullying was and the different forms it could take from actual students, they did not put forth a common definition around which the field and research participants could rally. That fact, combined with the students focusing on the forms and what they knew of the subject, did not focus on a comprehensive and workable conceptualization of the subject. Thus, the question remains:

Research Question 4a (sub-qualitative question): How do students define cyberbullying?

While definitions are a truly important foundation to any study, it is also necessary to gather rich qualitative data regarding actual student experiences that provide insightful details regarding the cyberbullying phenomenon:

Research Question 4b (sub-qualitative question): What experiences have they had with cyberbullying activity?

Gathering middle and high school students' experiences with cyberbullying is imperative to attaining a rich set of data that will help provide solid foundations to potential solutions to the undesirable and too often injurious behavior. While this study will work to balance potential psychological harms to students by asking them to share experiences in front of peers that may exploit their sharing or being in the same room as someone that may be a bully to them, it will provide questions regarding this research question in a follow-up anonymous and open-ended written survey.

Student words and thoughts demonstrate how cyberbullying affects their day-to-day lives. From the extant research literature it is apparent that technology has allowed peer networks to expand to a 24-hour a day, 7-day a week capacity. Some literature has indicated that these youngsters are so attached to participation in these networks that even if they are cyberbullied they do not want to detach in fear of being further isolated. However, there currently is not a clear understanding of where cyberbullying tends to take place and how cyberbullying affects the way they interact within their peer network:

Research Question 4c (sub-qualitative question): Where does cyberbullying take place?

Research Question 4d (sub-qualitative question): How has cyberbullying impacted their peer interactions?

Further, since students are using social technology to connect with peers they know in their physical world, it is also important to get student opinions on:

Research Question 4e (sub-qualitative question): How has cyberbullying activity impacted their perceptions of their school environment?

This is a key aspect of this study because cyberbullying, as is the case with bullying, has the potential to decrease the motivation to attend school and eventually worsen academic performance. Researchers have also found relationships between bullying and engaging in risky behaviors. Therefore, the following research question is appropriate for this study:

Research Question 4f (sub-qualitative question): How has cyberbullying activity impacted their participation in risky behaviors?

Much like the question about specific experience regarding cyberbullying and in the interest of balancing harms in human subjects research, information on this research question will be gained through the follow-up open-ended survey.

As a whole these qualitative research questions work to provide a rich description of the cyberbullying phenomenon directly through actual middle and high school student comments.

Research Question 5: To what extent and in what ways do qualitative data collection (i.e., focus groups and open-ended survey questions) among middle and high school students serve to contribute to a more comprehensive understanding of social technology use and cyberbullying for middle and high school students?

This question focuses on what the qualitative aspects—the focus groups and follow-up, open-ended questionnaire—have to offer to the study. In order to sufficiently examine this phenomenon, it will be necessary to explore not only student perceptions of a number of middle and high school students but to also gather student thoughts, ideas, and actual words regarding cyberbullying.

Mixed Methods Rationale

When conceptualizing a study, it is important to base the research design around the core research questions and think about the best way to answer those questions. In the case of these particular questions, research questions 1-3 clearly have quantitative aspects that lean towards finding relationships between variables and among constructs developed from multiple variables. Other questions, like research questions 4a-f, call for descriptions, the actual words, and points of view of the actual participants that lean towards the qualitative methodology. To create a comprehensive study which will produce an effective data set a mixed methods study design was selected.

Mixed methods research is an appropriate methodological choice if it is the most suitable way to answer the research questions of interest (Tashakkori & Teddlie, 2003) and when the qualitative or quantitative approach alone cannot adequately address the research problems to be addressed (Creswell, 2009). This type of research design works for this study because it answers the research questions posed by allowing data to emerge that speaks to determining frequency, identifying personal and situational characteristics, and exploring key relationships among variables within a large sample of the population, and then probing deeply into those findings by gathering student perceptions of cyberbullying, along with how and why those key relationships take place.

Mixed methods approaches have many strengths, which make them ideal to use in many research settings. At the most basic level, using quantitative methods allows for breadth and using qualitative methods allows for depth (Tashakkori & Teddlie, 2003). Essentially, using both quantitative and qualitative methods in a study provides for qualitative findings to give meaning to quantitative numbers and for numbers to add to the precision of the research (Johnson & Onwuegbuzie, 2004). By incorporating both types of methods it is possible to decrease the weaknesses inherent in both types of methods separately (Bryman, 2007; Denscombe, 2008) as it allows for the qualitative component to validate the quantitative aspect by giving further explanation and the chance to elaborate on the initial findings

(Creswell, 2009; Creswell, Clark, Gutmann, & Hanson, 2003; Johnson, Onwuegbuzie, & Turner, 2007). This, in turn, improves the accuracy of the data (Denscombe, 2008) to give researchers greater confidence in their findings as it decreases the chances of validity threats (Johnson, Onwuegbuzie, & Turner, 2007) such as instrument fidelity (Johnson & Onwuegbuzie, 2004).

Complementary quantitative and qualitative data generate a more complete picture of the phenomenon (Denscombe, 2008; Morse, 2003) with rich, meaningful answers (Johnson, Onwuegbuzie, & Turner, 2007) that disentangle intricate relationships (Sosulski & Lawrence, 2008) and bring to light insights that might not otherwise be apparent (Bryman, 2007). A mixed method approach allows the researcher to layer a large body of quantitative data with in-depth qualitative data. The qualitative data that was collected adds to the understanding of the initial quantitative data. Together, the information gathered in this study created a comprehensive picture of the cyberbullying phenomenon. However, there are some drawbacks to a mixed methods approach that merit attention.

Mixed methods approaches have several advantages but entail some limitations. First, significant time is needed to collect and analyze data, especially when the quantitative and qualitative components are given equal weight in the study design (Creswell, 2009). Mixed methods research studies are often very expensive (Johnson & Onwuegbuzie, 2004) and produce large volumes of data (Creswell, 2009) that require multiple variously trained and experienced researchers (Creswell, 2009; Johnson & Onwuegbuzie, 2004). This mixed methods study was possible to carryout due to the fact that the quantitative aspect had already been completed. However, a substantial amount of quantitative and qualitative data was analyzed which required a long period of time to review and analyze and necessitated mentoring by experienced researchers in the field.

Another barrier in the mixed methods research field is the fact that quantitative and qualitative methodologies are seen as fundamentally incompatible due to their different associated worldviews. The field of mixed methods research designs is still developing, and major epistemological and paradigmatic issues are still being debated (Jang, McDougall, Pollon, Herbert, & Russell, 2008; Tashakkori & Creswell, 2007). In reading this book it is necessary to be aware of the philosophical framework that is guiding the study at hand (Greene,

2008). While differences between quantitative and qualitative methodology are often highlighted, they do share many commonalities. For example, they both hinge on the collection of empirical observations, incorporate safeguards to increase validity, and have a process to them that includes describing the data, constructing an explanatory argument, and speculating as to why relationships found within observed data occur (Bazeley, 2002; Johnson & Onwuegbuzie, 2004).

Both quantitative and qualitative researchers tend to overlook the philosophical issues within their chosen methodological paradigm. Quantitative researchers traditionally come from a positivist/post-positivist background that entertains a rather narrow definition of science. This definition tends to focus on the strength of objectivity in identifying and assessing causes that influence outcomes, even though researchers make constant choices throughout the study based in their past experiences regarding the construction of instruments, choosing tests, and creating constructs of variables (Creswell, 2009; Johnson & Onwuegbuzie, 2004). Qualitative research traditionally comes from the relativist or constructivist background that focuses on the constructed reality of participant views which make it difficult to judge quality as it focuses on a subjective reality (Creswell, 2009; Johnson & Onwuegbuzie, 2004).

As indicated earlier in this section, it is important to be conscious of the philosophical assumptions underlying the chosen framework. Before 1950, a number of respected researchers (e.g., the 1939 Hawthorne Studies and the 1941 Yankee City Study) used mixed methods designs without real controversy. However, between 1950 and 1970 the quantitative field began to focus on the weaknesses of positivism and turned towards post-positivism as a remedy. During this time numerous highly regarded mixed methods studies were conducted (e.g., 1956—End of the World Cults; 1969—Stanford Prison Study), but the practice still had not become a distinct field of study. Between 1970 and 1990 mixed methods issues garnered increased attention as qualitative methods and constructivism grew in popularity among social scientists. As constructivists argued for a space in the methodological realm, they took a stance that they were not only different from the postpositivists but were superior in many respects. This, in turn, provided space for arguments over paradigm purity, which made themselves evident in the paradigm wars of the 1980s—

and most notably, the advent of the incompatibility thesis that stated that due to the divergent epistemological backgrounds of each type of methodology the act of mixing them was "wrong" and could only result in failure. The period including 1990 to the present has provided researchers with the emergence of *pragmatism* as the working paradigm, the compatibility thesis, and textbooks that establish mixed methods research as a separate field (Tashakkori & Teddlie, 2003).

Due to the paradigm wars and incompatibility thesis, mixed methods studies must defend their choice and make paradigmatic choices apparent to readers. As for paradigmatic choices, this study will take the position that mixed methods research is to be considered the third major paradigm (Denscombe, 2008; Johnson, Onwuegbuzie, & Turner, 2007). Further, the qualitative and quantitative methodologies are viewed as being compatible, and can work together to generate a more complete picture of the cyberbullying phenomenon. While post-positivism and constructivism have their respective strengths this study will operate under the principal assumptions of pragmatism. Pragmatism focuses on real world experiences and consequences (Johnson & Onwuegbuzie, 2004), and accepts both qualitative and quantitative methods and focuses on using whichever methods allow for the most complete understanding (Creswell, 2009). Pragmatism focuses on the idea that different theories—such as post-positivism and constructivism—have aspects that can be helpful when combined, as well as that "knowledge is both constructed and based on reality of the world we experiment and live in" (Johnson & Onwuegbuzie, 2004). This is important to this study as it features not only quantitative survey data, but participant's views on the cyberbullying phenomenon as well.

A Sequential Explanatory Mixed Methods Design

This study falls under the category of a sequential explanatory mixed methods design. Creswell (2009) writes that "sequential mixed methods procedures are those in which the researcher seeks to elaborate on or expand on the findings of one method with another method" (p. 14). Creswell (2008) also defines an explanatory mixed methods design as consisting of "first collecting quantitative data and then collecting qualitative data to help explain or elaborate on the quantitative results" (p. 560). To best explain this type of design it is easiest to break apart the terms to do so. First, this study employed both quantitative and qualitative measures. This study utilized quantitative survey data and qualitative focus groups and open-ended questionnaire, which will be further detailed in the next section. Using both survey data and focus group data created an environment for a mixed methods design.

The sequential design was chosen because it allows the quantitative and qualitative data collection to be conducted separately. This brings one of the main strengths of mixed methods designs to the forefront as it allows for the ability to validate findings and dig into key relationships from the initial component in the follow-up component. The remaining term “explanatory” refers to the quantitative aspect being conducted first in the sequence, with a follow-up qualitative component. What makes this design possible for this study is that there is extant literature available from which the research questions can be derived. From the literature it was determined that much of the empirical study of the cyberbullying phenomenon was inconclusive and needed further study to determine significance. As there is such information available, there was little need to explore qualitatively first to find important variables and relationships to test. Therefore, conducting the quantitative aspect first was possible, and due to the circumstances (i.e., the quantitative data already being collected) fits well with the present study’s situation.

Further, completing the mixed methods designs study in a sequential explanatory way illuminated key relationships and provided a more comprehensive understanding of the initial quantitative findings. Thus, the study would be considered an explanatory design as it focused on the quantitative component being conducted first and used the qualitative component to further explain some of the key findings. The next section will detail the data collection process and the statistical analysis processes employed for this study.

To summarize, a mixed methods approach to studying the cyberbullying phenomenon is appropriate for this study as it first and foremost works to answer the research questions presented. Further, even though this study yielded a substantial amount of data, reviewing quantitative survey data regarding the perceptions of thousands of middle and high school students on cyberbullying activity and qualitatively digging deeper provided the study with a rich data set that gives a much fuller picture of the cyberbullying phenomenon than any existing study.

DATA COLLECTION AND ANALYSIS

This section speaks to the actual quantitative and qualitative data collection and analysis involved in this study. This section begins by discussing the population, the sample, and the participant recruitment process for the quantitative and qualitative aspects of the study. Then, it will turn towards in-depth descriptions of the quantitative data collection and analysis process, the qualitative data collection and analysis process, and finally sets forth how the study is viewed as an interconnected whole.

Population, Sample, and Participant Recruitment

While cyberbullying can take place among all ages, in many places, and at most any time, this research focuses on middle and high school students. Middle and high school students are some of the most rampant users of new types of social technology and are likely to utilize even newer technologies as they emerge (boyd, 2008; Ito et al., 2010). Thus, many individuals within this population are likely to use the tools that allow for participation in cyberbullying activity. Further, individuals in this population share the same spaces during a time when children are becoming young men and women, learning the terms of acceptable behavior, learning social norms, pushing terms of acceptable behavior, negotiating social norms, and relying heavily on their peer networks (boyd, 2007b; Hinduja & Patchin, 2009; Ito et al., 2008; Ito et al., 2010; Williams and Merten, 2008; Varjas, Henrich, & Meyers, 2009).

Due to inherited circumstances from the quantitative aspect of the study, which will be discussed in the next section, as well as this being a self-funded study, the sample area is limited to middle and high school students aged 12-18 who attended schools that participated in the *Safe Schools and Healthy Students Program* in 2009. This means the survey responses used in the analysis come from a non-random pool of participants. Thus, results from this survey will not reflect a random sample from the general area of the study location, and be limited to those individuals whose schools participated in the program in 2009. In this particular study every school that took part in the program in 2009 (n=26) was asked to have their students take the Youth Risk Behavior Survey (YRBS). For the qualitative aspect of this study, focus groups were conducted at a small subset (n=2) of the surveyed schools. The initial university Criminal Justice department researchers retained a relationship with some of the schools in the sample, giving further access to an occasional, non-representative access to qualitative data collection. Another middle school (n=1) outside of the *Safe Schools Healthy Students Program* was added to the sample to enhance the number of cases for analysis.

The participants in both the qualitative and quantitative portions of the study reside in a Midwest city, hereafter referred to as "research location." The research location is an urban metropolis with over 950,000 people. According the U.S. Census Bureau, 25.1% of the residents are under the age of 18 and 51.8% are female. The racial makeup of the area is illustrated in Table 6.

Table 6: *Race in the Research Location*

Race	Percentage
White	68.3%
Black	25.7%
Asian	3.2%
Reporting 2+ Races	1.8%
American Indian	0.9%
Native Hawaiian/Other Pacific Islander	0.1%

Note. 12.2% reported having a Hispanic or Latino origin

In the research location 80.2% of those over the age of 25 are high school graduates and 23.6% over the age of 25 have a bachelor's degree. Research location residents have a median household income of $45,902 and 17% of residents live below the poverty line.

Quantitative Data Collection

An explanatory mixed methods study requires an initial quantitative component to be followed by a qualitative component. An anonymous survey was an appropriate choice for the quantitative aspect of the study as it can be used for descriptive, exploratory, and explanatory purposes on a potentially large scale where individuals are the unit of analysis (Maxfield & Babbie, 2009). Surveys are common when measuring victimization (e.g., National Crime Victimization Survey) and when asking individuals to self-report on why they commit delinquent acts (Maxfield & Babbie, 2009). Since this study focused on incidence, victimization, perpetration, and participation in risky behaviors, including cyberbullying activity, a survey was a natural choice for accomplishing these objectives.

This study utilized data from a survey that has already been collected. This existing data set has been collected by way of the YRBS that had been adapted from its original form. The YRBS is both a valid and reliable survey instrument (Brener, Collins, Kann, Warren, & Williams, 1995). The original YRBS asks questions that are quite inclusive and wide-ranging (e.g., bike safety, car safety, carrying weapons, bullying behavior, involvement in physical altercations, depression, suicide, tobacco use, alcohol use, drug use, sexual intercourse, dietary behaviors). The objective of the study in which the data were collected was specific to risky behaviors that affected the school environment (e.g., bullying behavior, physical altercations, carrying weapons) and smoking, drug use, and alcohol use. Thus, the original YRBS was adapted by shortening the original questionnaire to disregard questions regarding general risky behavior (i.e., bike safety, car safety, sexual intercourse, dietary behaviors, etc.). The adapted survey also added questions regarding cyberbullying asking participants about frequency of social technology (defined as social networking sites and chat rooms) use, frequency of cyberbullying victimization (defined as being in a social networking site or chat room), and frequency of cyberbullying perpetration (defined as making fun of or telling lies about other students using email, instant messaging or social networking sites). These three questions were not piloted prior to survey distribution.

Data were collected in February and March of 2009 by classroom teachers within the sample by way of the YRBS (see Appendix A) and was compiled by trained personnel. As stated previously the original researchers only had access to the schools in the research location that participated in the *Safe Schools and Healthy Students Program*, which was only a fraction of the middle and high schools in the county. The non-random survey data were collected once, and researchers gathered 3,403 responses from a total population of 11,086 for a response rate of 30.7%. However, it is important to note that this response rate was not representative of a mass refusal of survey completion by participants. Instead, there were some schools that did not participate even though they had agreed to do so, and did not offer the survey to their students via paper or online means. Other schools produced more survey results than others, and with the latter noting problems with logistical matters (i.e., getting students computer access or setting aside time to take the survey, which would reduce teacher-student time).

Initial Quantitative Data Analysis

In a sequential explanatory mixed methods study, protocol indicates that researchers analyze quantitative data first (Creswell, 2009). The findings from the initial quantitative analysis thereby inform the qualitative data collection and are further explored in conjunction with the qualitative findings later in the process. This section will examine items pertinent to the initial quantitative data analysis process. First, the variables of interest will be discussed and the relevant independent and dependent variables will be specified. Then, the rationale for choosing specific statistical tests for the quantitative data analysis process will be provided.

The Youth Risk Behavior Survey (YRBS) yielded many variables that helped to further describe the cyberbullying phenomenon. Some of these variables were viewed as independent variables, some as dependent variables, and some existed as both independent and dependent variables in various hypothesized causal sequences. The main independent variables that were utilized in this study revolved around demographic survey items. These demographic items include grade, age, sex and race.

Key variables in this study revolved specifically around the cyberbullying phenomenon. These variables included how often middle and high school students used social network sites, how often they had been victims of cyberbullying, and how often they had cyberbullied others. These cyberbullying variables existed either as independent variables or dependent variables given the circumstance. For example, in this study these variables can be seen as independent variables as they can potentially influence risk-taking behaviors and affect school safety perceptions. Conversely, these cyberbullying variables can be seen as dependent variables as they have the potential to be influenced by the independent demographic variables of grade, age, sex, and race.

One of the strengths of the YRBS was that it measured both risk-taking behaviors and perceptions of those behaviors, as well as items that pertained to school safety. These items were integral to understanding how often students engaged in risky behaviors (e.g., alcohol, cigarettes, drugs, etc.), how they perceived these risky behaviors as affecting them, and how safe they viewed their school environment to be. In this study these items were considered as dependent variables as they were viewed as outcome variables in connection to independent influencing cyberbullying variables such as social network use and engagement in cyberbullying behaviors (i.e., perpetration and victimization).

Data were prepared for SPSS and were analyzed using both descriptive and inferential statistics. Descriptive statistics are used in quantitative analysis to "summarize, organize, and simplify data" (Gravetter & Wallnau, 2007, p. 6). In the case of this study, descriptive statistics were run on all variables to provide an understanding of frequency. In contrast, inferential statistics are used in quantitative analysis "to study samples and then make generalizations about the populations from which they were selected" (Gravetter & Wallnau, 2007, p. 7). Inferential statistics were used to identify key relationships and make predictions that are generalizable. Statistical testing is an iterative process. This study used an incrementally increasing level of sophistication to specify the nature and statistical significance of important relationships between variables and among sets of variables. In some cases, sets of variables were aggregated to create factors (e.g., drugs, violence, etc.). Factors can be created either via statistically driven approaches such as factor analysis or conceptually driven. In this analysis, factors were created following theoretically driven approaches and confirmed through goodness of fit statistics.

Four inferential statistical tests were conducted during the initial quantitative analysis aspect of this study, namely: analysis of variance (ANOVA), correlation, independent sample t-tests, and ordinary least squares regression. First, ANOVA was conducted to determine the significance of group differences within a single variable and between multiple independent variables. ANOVA indicated whether statistically significant variance was present for the population with respect to a given variable. Correlation tests were conducted to identify key relationships between pairs of variables. ANOVA and correlation allowed for an understanding of key variables and key relationships within sets of variables that convey relationships requiring further assessment. Next, independent samples t-tests were conducted to determine the nature of the relationship and if path variables were concurrent (e.g., when one variable increases the other does as well) or divergent (e.g., when one variable increases the other decreases). Based on these findings a regression model can be formatted. The final statistical test in this analysis was multiple regression so that nature and direction between many of the variables could be specified. Further, multiple regression was used to determine what combination can best explain the variance associated with the dependent variables.

After the iterative statistical process was completed, findings were reviewed and applied toward the mixed methods design. These quantitative findings worked to inform the qualitative-based research questions and add focus-areas to the proposed qualitative data collection protocols.

Qualitative Data Collection

After the survey data were analyzed the findings were used to construct questions for the qualitative focus group sessions. Focus groups are an appropriate choice when the research calls for looking at differences in perspective, when uncovering factors that influence behaviors, when actual participant comments will add to the study, and especially in enhancing the quantitative data (Krueger & Casey, 2000). In the case of this study this was an appropriate choice as its focus was to uncover perceptions around cyberbullying, gather actual student comments regarding cyberbullying, and specifically uncover relationships related to the quantitative findings.

Focus groups are also an appropriate method of qualitative data collection when children are the participants. Heary and Hennessy (2002) found that focus groups give more power to youth perceptions as the process removes the adult-child hierarchical relationship as it puts the participant at the center as expert. This setting likely elicits more responses from children than interviews would. Focus groups have also recently been utilized by those researchers seeking qualitative answers to cyberbullying questions.

While much of the limited existing research on cyberbullying has been quantitative in nature, researchers have begun to use focus groups for studying issues related to cyberbullying. Vandebosch and VanCleemput (2008) conducted 53 focus groups with 279 students (142 males/137 females; mean age of 14.1) to work through the conceptualization issues revolving around cyberbullying to help define what cyberbullying actually is for students that deal with cyberbullying problems. Agatston, Kowalski, and Limber (2007) used focus groups with 150 students in middle and high schools with diverse socioeconomic status (note that the number of focus groups was not specified). Agatston et al. asked questions that looked for understanding around how familiar students were with technology, how many owned cell phones, how many had Internet access at home, who saw cyberbullying as a problem, where cyberbullying takes place, to whom students who experience cyberbullying actually tells about the experience, and which strategies they use to deal with this kind of bullying.

Mishna, Saini, and Solomon (2009) also used focused groups, conducting 7 focus groups among 30 students in the 5th-8th grades. To address concerns about breaking confidentiality and putting students in awkward positions of revealing personal experiences in front of peers, they did not ask participants about their own experiences specifically. Instead they asked participants their views of cyberbullying, how often they think it occurs, what form it usually takes, who does the cyberbullying, who is cyberbullied, who knows about the cyberbullying, and whom they tell about it. While this is not ideal for qualitative research as it does not give the rich participant responses and leans towards superficial data, it does protect the students that are participating in the focus groups. This is an important aspect of any research study as it is imperative to "weigh the potential benefits from doing research against the possibility of harm to the people being studied" (Maxfield & Babbie, 2009, pp. 27-8). Thus, a focus group session with an anonymous follow-up individual cyberbullying exercise was considered an ideal way for this particular study to balance the benefits and harms of the study.

Horner (2000) indicates that focus groups are very useful with youth—especially middle school students—as the process allows the researcher "to gather detailed information about participants' experiences, insights, or beliefs about a selected topic" (p. 570). However, there are also limitations with focus groups overall, and with using focus groups with youth in particular. Heary and Hennessy (2002) indicate that individuals in the focus group may be subject to in-group intimidation and more likely to adopt their fellow focus group members' perspectives as anonymity is compromised. Thus, the authors advise that the optimal group size hovers around 4-5, to keep the sessions less than sixty minutes, have participants of the same gender in a group to avoid trying to impress or feel embarrassed among the opposite gender, and to weigh whether the individuals gathered should be of the same friendship group or not.

This study's focus groups aimed to have group sizes between 4-5 and keep gender separated in focus group sessions when it was possible. In an attempt to try to keep cyberbullies and cyberbully victims in different groups to avoid victim uneasiness, school staff were consulted to determine focus group makeup. To balance potential benefits with potential harm to participants the protocol for this study, like Mishna et al. (2009), did not ask participants to reveal personal, specific experiences during the focus groups (see Appendix B). As outlined above, some questions may be difficult to answer for some individuals in a group—especially if cyberbullies bully their own friendship group (which is always possible), cyberbullies and cyberbully victims unknowingly get selected to be in the same focus group, or relevant experiences are particularly embarrassing.

However, these experiences were integral for furthering the study of cyberbullying and the ultimate goal of providing solutions to the cyberbullying phenomenon with firm foundations in research. Thus, during this study's focus group period there was a fifteen-minute span of time at the end of the focus group session where students had the opportunity to expound on their previous answers or private thoughts in an open-ended questionnaire (see Appendix C). This open-ended questionnaire also asked for feelings regarding the quantitative findings around risky behaviors associated with cyberbullying. Before students left the focus group session they were given a handout that had information about what to do if they had been victims of cyberbullying, and where to turn in case they needed help with risky behaviors (e.g., alcohol, drugs, school violence).

As juveniles are a special, legally protected population, particular care was taken in regards to attaining consent from parents/guardians and making sure the teenagers themselves wanted to participate. Participation was entirely voluntary, and confidentiality was covered during the session as well. It is also important to note that while focus groups were being conducted at schools a number of school staff that helped to schedule the sessions expressed interest in participating in focus groups and interviews to give their side of the cyberbullying own story. To meet their needs an IRB amendment was applied for and granted before the school staff focus groups and interviews took place.

One focus group session with three individuals and two individual interviews featuring school staff were conducted. Please see Appendix D for the school staff interview guide.

Initial Qualitative Data Analysis

The focus group data were collected, transcribed, and prepared for coding to identify major themes. Once themes are detected the real words of the focus group participants were segmented by theme to determine major findings. While Nvivo was a possibility for analyzing qualitative data, with relatively fewer focus groups to analyze it was more useful to become closer with the data by developing and following a manual coding system. This manual coding system is depicted in Table 7.

Table 7: ***Process of Qualitative Data Analysis***

Step	Process
1	Read all focus group transcripts to get a sense of the whole
2	Read one transcript in-depth, noting potential topics
3	Entered topics from Step 2 into a list
4	Analyze all transcripts coding for topics
5	Reviewed initial transcripts to look for later topics
6	Finalized topic list
7	Pasted pertinent participant quotes related to the topic list
8	Generated a description of the cyberbullying phenomenon

Reviewing the Quantitative and Qualitative Findings Together

Once the quantitative and qualitative data were independently analyzed, the final aspect of mixing the methods took place as both forms of data were interpreted together. The first mixing took place when quantitative findings were used to inform the qualitative research questions, as well as the focus group and follow-up open-ended qualitative survey questions. Both quantitative findings (by way of SPSS outputs) and qualitative findings (files with emerging themes present in focus groups and follow-up open-ended survey) were leveraged to address the research questions. Potential answers to the research questions were then coded in both sets and merged to create a final, comprehensive findings report. Students who participated in focus group sessions in 2011 may not have been the same individuals that took the YRBS in 2009 due to the expanse in time and logistics given particular school participation. Given this data discontinuity, quantitative YRBS results and the qualitative focus group data are seen as complimentary to one another and not necessarily derived from the same data pool.

Data Collection and Analysis Summary

This study was conducted as a sequential explanatory mixed method design. This design is depicted in Figure 1.

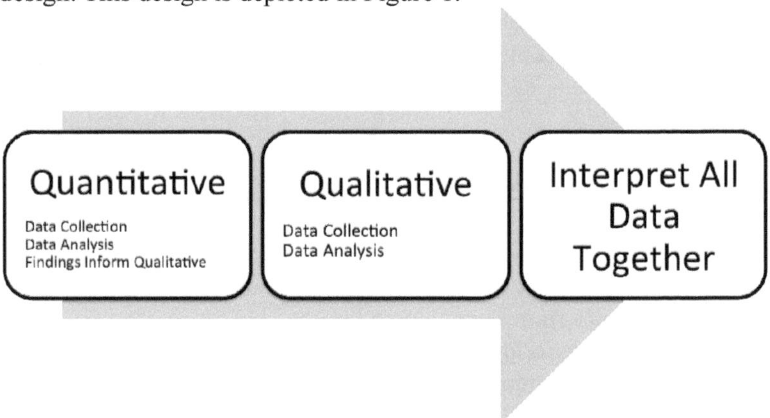

Figure 1. **Study Design. This figure illustrates how this study was conducted.**

The study started with a quantitative element and then moved towards a qualitative element by starting with the 2009 YRBS and moving towards qualitative focus groups. Using the quantitative aspect to inform focus group questions and follow-up questionnaire items, focus groups were conducted with a short period of time allowed at the end of them set aside for the completion of the follow-up questionnaire. This questionnaire focused on personal experiences and items they may not have felt comfortable sharing in a group. After these sessions were completed, data were transcribed and analyzed to reveal common themes. In the final aspect of the study—and the second time methods were mixed—findings from the quantitative survey and from the qualitative focus groups were analyzed together to reveal a comprehensive data set that spoke to the cyberbullying phenomenon.

STUDY LIMITATIONS

In this section the limitations of choosing a mixed methods approach will be briefly reiterated, and then the particular limitations associated with the quantitative and qualitative aspects of the study will be set forth in some detail.

Mixed Methods—General

As discussed in previous sections, a significant amount of time and resources are needed to do a true mixed methods design study. Often, the amount of data produced and experience required to comprehend it all make it difficult for a single researcher to carry out a mixed methods design research project. While analyzing a quantitative data set, collecting qualitative data, and analyzing qualitative data required a significant amount time and effort, it made for a worthwhile comprehensive study of the cyberbullying phenomenon. Undertaking a mixed methods study for this research project would not have been feasible if the data for the quantitative survey had not already been collected. Designing, piloting, adapting, and administering surveys to over 3,000 respondents would have taken months (if not years) on a limited budget and conventional time schedule.

Quantitative Aspect

Utilizing secondary data means that one has no control over how the survey instrument was constructed or how survey data were actually collected. For example, race is an oft-neglected variable in cyberbullying research and capturing the race of survey participants accurately would have enhanced the explanatory power of the analysis materially. However, the survey instrument allowed students to select multiple responses when selecting race. While this gives students the opportunity to select the different parts of their race, it makes calculating meaningful responses in this category difficult.

A number of questions (e.g., depression, suicide, academic performance, etc.) were omitted from the original YRBS that would have been useful in this analysis. This was an artifact of the act of tailoring the survey to meet their study's purpose (i.e., school safety and risky behavior) and reflected the need to condense the original YRBS to increase participation rates. Also, in the adaptation process three questions were added regarding cyberbullying that were not piloted. It would have been useful to pilot these questions to make sure they were on target for gaining the most information regarding the phenomenon. The first of the three questions asked about frequency of use regarding social network sites and chat rooms. The second of the three questions asked if the student had been a victim of cyberbullying in these venues (social network sites and chat rooms), while the third question asked if individuals made fun of or told lies about other students using email, instant messaging, or social networking sites (see Appendix A for the YRBS).

These questions are problematic for a few reasons. The first two questions have a limiting sense to them as they mention social network sites and chat rooms when cyberbullying can and does take place in other venues. Second, the question regarding victimization is limited to the specified venues. The most troubling though, is the third question that is quite different from the other two in that it defines cyberbullying just as making fun or telling lies about someone and it could potentially confuse student participants and disconnect within the data in that it extends where the cyberbullying can take place to email and instant messaging, while not mentioning the chat rooms from the previous two questions.

Another limitation to the quantitative aspect is that it is often difficult to determine causality from survey data. Maxfield and Babbie (2009) write that there are three criteria to causality—namely, the cause preceding the effect, the cause and effect occurring together, and the observed correlation can not be explained by another variable. Survey data provided frequency of cyberbullying victimization and perpetration, as well as demographic variables associated with these items. These data also provided information to examine if relationships exist between those that indicate participation in cyberbullying behavior and partaking in risky behavior (i.e., bringing weapons to school, drinking alcohol, taking drugs, etc.) and feelings of school safety. However, from this survey, we were not able to decipher causality. For example, the quantitative findings showed that there was a significant relationship between risky behavior and cyberbullying activity. However, we were not able to determine if middle and high school students partake in risky behaviors because of the stress of participating in cyberbullying behavior, or rather if participating in cyberbullying behavior puts them into a peer group where these risky behaviors are more commonplace. Thus, we cannot be certain that cyberbullying behavior precedes the risky behavior, that these items even occur together, or that they cannot be explained by another variable. The qualitative aspect was therefore needed to further define relationships uncovered in the quantitative survey data.

A final limitation is the sample for the quantitative aspect. The sample was not randomly drawn and its aim was to survey as many middle and high school students as possible from the *Safe Schools and Healthy Students Program* which is only a fraction of schools in the research location. Thus, this is not a representative sample of middle and high school students in the research location or the United States; consequently, reported findings cannot be generalized to a larger entity than those that are indicative of the program. Rather, it pertains to the perspectives of a large number of middle and high school students who attend schools that participated in the *Safe Schools Healthy Choices Initiative* in the research location area in 2009. While not a perfect dataset by any means, an asset of these data is the fact that it provided responses from a large number of middle and high school students—larger than the majority of other cyberbullying studies located in the extant literature review—of teenage students regarding engagement in risky and cyberbullying behavior.

Qualitative Aspect

There were several limitations associated with the qualitative aspect of the research study. First, schools were not randomly selected to participate in the focus group sections. Instead we approached the researchers who conducted the YRBS to gain an understanding of which schools would be open to having further research conducted at their respective sites. Also, with the limited time and resources available for this study, only four student focus groups were conducted, and one school staff focus group, and two school staff interviews at three schools were carried out. The most important thing to realize about qualitative research is its purpose. According to Creswell (2008), qualitative inquiry's intent is not to generalize or hypothesize to a population, but rather to develop an in-depth exploration of a central phenomenon. The purpose of using qualitative research in this study was to provide middle and high school students' actual words and perspectives on the cyberbullying phenomenon, which, in turn, created a more comprehensive study.

As cited earlier, focus groups are often subject to in-group intimidation where group members will adopt other group member perspectives even if they do not reflect their true feelings. However, focus groups were selected for the group dynamic that allowed one to feed off another to share things they might not have thought of in an interview situation. It was also selected to help bridge the gap between adults and teenagers and diminish the power differential sometimes felt by teenagers in an interview situation. A different issue that cyberbullying researchers have struggled with when doing focus groups is balancing harms to students by asking rather vague questions about cyberbullying and about related conceptualization items, but not getting actual experiences. This can lead to the potential for superficial data when in-depth study is needed to provide truly workable solutions to this vast problem. This study adhered to the common practice of not asking for personal experiences during the focus group discussion and incorporated the use of an anonymous, follow-up open-ended questionnaire that asked students to share these experiences. As this study looked for connections with risky behaviors (e.g., drug and alcohol use) it was important that the questionnaire was anonymous and that students, on their way out of the focus group session, were given a place to turn to if they are victims of cyberbullying and places they could get help if they are having problems with drugs and alcohol.

QUALITY CONTROL MEASURES

To maintain internal reliability in light of the aforementioned limitations, this study included measures to ensure quality control. As indicated earlier, taking on an existing data set as part of a research project means that you had no control over how the data collection instrument was constructed or how data was actually collected. As surveys are stronger on reliability than on validity, the qualitative component aided in the determination if the actual answers in the survey reflected options and true feelings of the student participants.

As qualitative focus groups are an additive aspect from the original data, we had more control over how the groups were conducted. For example, it was pertinent to run the focus groups with two moderators so that one could run the focus group while the other took notes if recording devices failed, and would step in if clarity was needed. To make certain that participant comments were fully realized, the lead moderator asked clarifying questions to ensure comments were clearly understood (Krueger & Casey, 2000). The moderator also summarized comments heard and asked participants if they agreed at the end of each question section (Krueger & Casey, 2000). Qualitative validity focuses on checking the accuracy of the findings. To ensure accuracy we conducted transcript checks, utilized thick description, had an external auditor, reflected on our role and biases, and presented both positive and negative data in our results.

CHAPTER SUMMARY

Due to a methodologically varied set of research questions that arose from gaps in literature and access to data sets (i.e., 2009 YRBS), a sequential explanatory mixed method design was selected for this study. This study design featured a quantitative aspect that surveyed a large number of middle and high school students regarding risky behavior, social technology use, and cyberbullying engagement (i.e., perpetration and victimization). After this data was collected it was analyzed to reveal key relationships and questions that needed further explanation through qualitative focus groups and interviews. Findings from the study are depicted in subsequent chapters.

CHAPTER 4

Social Technology Use and Frequency of Bullying Behavior

> "Facebook is where everything happens."--Female high school student

In the survey students were asked how often they used MySpace, Facebook, chat rooms, or other social network sites. They were also asked about their participation in cyberbullying behavior. This chapter uses both YRBS and focus group data to explain social technology use and bullying behavior among the middle and high school youth in our study.

SOCIAL TECHNOLOGY USE

A majority of students (55%) reported using these sites regularly (either every day or a few times per week). A smaller amount of students (11.5%) indicated mild usage (a few times per month), while 8.3% cited only using these kinds of sites a few times per year. Just over one quarter of students never used these venues. Social network usage is depicted in Table 8.

Table 8: ***Social Network Usage***

Frequency	Usage (n)	Valid %
Never	854	25.4%
A few times per year	277	8.3%
A few times per month	387	11.5%
A few times per week	808	24.1%
Every day	1,030	30.7%

With quantitative analysis revealing a majority of students using social network sites, focus group questions were tailored to dig deeper into how students were using social technology. Students acknowledged using a variety of social technology tools. The social network site, Facebook, and texting were the two most commonly cited communication channels among the participants. Students also mentioned using video chat (e.g., Skype), Xbox Live, and chat programs offered through email clients (e.g., Gmail). Still used, but far less frequently, was conventional email. Generally, students indicated that they only sent emails around once or a few times per week. Students also indicated that email was something that they used to interact with adults (e.g., older family members). Both males and females reported using multiple social technologies, with males reporting use of gaming systems such as Xbox Live more frequently than females.

Use of Facebook

Facebook was reported as one of the most frequently employed tools which suggested questions about the ways students used this application. Students reported having between 93 and 4,000 friends, with most students reporting several hundred friends. For the most part students knew exactly (or very nearly) how many friends they had, and indicated that they knew everyone on their friend list or "normally saw each other." At the very least, they knew someone that knew them (e.g., friend of a friend, school network, etc.). One student said: "Well, like I know most of them. Not like you go up and talk to them if you saw them somewhere, but like I know who they are." Students are connected on Facebook to people they have close relationships with, but are also connected to many more whom they do not know as well. While they are on Facebook they mentioned that they like to use the chat feature with their friends, check notifications, update status messages, and look around other people's pages.

Students varied on the frequency with which they checked Facebook. Some said as little as 2-3 times per week, while others said 2-3 (e.g., morning and night) times per day. One student commented that she liked to check Facebook every 30 minutes. One student explained: "I just leave my page open, but if I sit down I stay on Facebook for 15 minutes." Like this student, others also indicated that after they got home from school (as use of the site was prohibited at school) they opened their Facebook page and left it open for the remainder of the evening.

Students also commented how Internet-connected tools—such as iPods and cell phones—allowed them to stay connected to Facebook more often. One student noted: "I guess I'm on it every day but that's because my iPod. I can have it on chat." It is fair to say that students have many Facebook friends, most of whom they know or at the very least know of. They use a variety of social technologies (e.g., Facebook, cell phones, email chat clients, video chat, xBox Live, etc.), but widespread peer use of Facebook makes it one of the most popular choices. Students tend to check Facebook often for notifications and to update their statuses regularly. Cell phones with Internet access, iPods with Wi-Fi, and home computers help to keep them connected and current.

Reasons for Social Technology Use

With students having so many access points (e.g., Facebook, texting, etc.) to their peer groups they can communicate whenever the inclination hits them. They cited various reasons for communicating with friends via social technologies. At the most basic level students indicated that they used Facebook and texted with friends when they were bored: "Sometimes my friends text me or sometimes I text them. When I text them it's just because I'm bored and I want to talk." When students were bored they talked about their hobbies (e.g., sports, music, etc.) and typically engaged with family and old friends.

They also used social technologies for school purposes: "If you miss school you can check what's due and see what you missed." While students often used social technologies for school purposes, it seems they also were likely to use it while doing homework as well: "Well, when I'm doing homework or sometimes when I'm bored I talk to them." Therefore, students utilize social technologies to get assignments when they miss school and while they are doing schoolwork at home, which could lead either to students helping one another with assignments or to provide further distraction from the homework task. Unfortunately, social technology tools are not only used for positive behaviors—such as chatting about school homework assignments—but also used for engaging in cyberbullying activity with their fellow classmates.

CYBERBULLYING ACTIVITY

YRBS results revealed that a number of students reported participating in cyberbullying activity. A majority of students (89%) had never been victimized by a cyberbullying act. However, 1.4% of students who took the survey reported being victimized every day, and 1.9% of these students reported being victimized a few times a week, respectively. The largest percentage of students (5.3%) who were victimized by cyberbullying indicated that they were victimized a few times per year. Cyberbullying victimization is shown in Table 9.

Table 9: *Cyberbullying Victimization*

Frequency	Victimization (n)	Valid %
Never	2,951	88.8%
A few times per year	176	5.3%
A few times per month	83	2.5%
A few times per week	62	1.9%
Every day	49	1.4%

A large majority of students (80.4%) reported never perpetrating an act of cyberbullying. However, 3.5% indicated perpetrating cyberbullying acts a few times per week, while 3.9% did so a few times per month. The largest percentage of students (9.1%) who indicated some degree of perpetration indicated that they had cyberbullied another individual a few times per year. Cyberbullying perpetration rates are shown in Table 10.

Table 10: *Cyberbullying Perpetration*

Frequency	Perpetration (n)	Valid %
Never	2,646	80.4%
A few times per year	300	9.1%
A few times per month	129	3.9%
A few times per week	114	3.5%
Every day	97	2.9%

While a majority of students report using social network sites frequently, many students report not participating in cyberbullying activity as either a perpetrator or victim. However, just over 11% of respondents indicated that they were indeed victimized by cyberbullying behavior at least a few times a year. Within that 11%, 1.4% report being victimized every day, and 1.9% at least a few times every week. This is quite substantial given the frequency of victimization for these individuals. Perpetration of cyberbullying acts are more common than victimization, suggesting that a small number of victims may be disproportionately targeted by bullies in a cumulative or "piling-on" effect.

To gain a better understanding of cyberbullying behavior students were asked in the focus group sections how often it occurred. In a middle school focus group session the students were asked if cyberbullying happens a lot and, as a group, they replied "everyday." When this question was asked in another middle school focus group session the participants agreed with the other:

> **Female Focus Group Participant 1:** I think it's a lot.
>
> **Female Focus Group Participant 2:** I think it's serious.
>
> **Female Focus Group Participant 3:** Because some people end up killing themselves.

Students were aware that cyberbullying was happening often to peers in their school, and elsewhere around the world. They indicated that they thought cyberbullying was quite serious, as they had heard stories of fellow teenagers becoming depressed and taking their lives. However, they seemed somewhat removed from these stories, as they did not know anyone in their lives that was so depressed over a cyberbullying act who would take his/her life. However, they were aware that participation in cyberbullying activity was problematic and related to fighting, traditional bullying, and other risky behaviors.

Fighting, Traditional Bullying, and Perceptions of School Safety

The YRBS asked students multiple questions to assess their perceptions of fighting, traditional bullying, and school safety. Students we asked how often in the past 12 months they were harassed, picked on, or bullied so much that they felt unsafe at school. Nearly 16% of students reported being bullied in the past year to the point where they felt unsafe at school. Data indicate that nearly 15% of students missed at least one of the past 30 days of school because they felt unsafe during their school day (i.e., on the way to school, while at school, or on the way home from school). Students were also asked how often they brought a weapon (e.g., gun, knife, or club) onto school property. Approximately 5% of student indicated that they had brought a weapon to school over the past 30 days. While a majority of students (71.2%)

reported that they had not engaged in a fight on school property over the past 12 months, nearly 15% reported fighting at least once, 8.5% reported fighting 2-3 times, and nearly 6% reported fighting 4 or more times during the past 12 months.

A number of YRBS questions pertained to drug use and the perceived risk of drug use. Students were asked about smoking cigarettes, drinking alcohol, smoking marijuana, taking prescription drugs, and using hard drugs (e.g., cocaine, crack, methamphetamines, ecstasy, or heroin). After being asked how often they partook in the behavior (e.g., smoking cigarettes, drinking alcohol, etc.) students were asked how much they thought people risk harming themselves (physically and in other ways) if they participate in that behavior (e.g., smoking 1-2 packs a day, drinking 1-2 drinks a day). The majority of students (92%) reported not smoking cigarettes in the past 30 days, with nearly half (48.6%) of students perceiving the act of smoking as being moderately risky or higher. The majority of students (80%) reported not drinking alcohol in the past 30 days, with 30% believing that drinking is moderately risky or higher. Table 11 depicts self-reported illegal drug usage.

Table 11: ***Drug Usage***

Frequency	Marijuana (past 30 days)	Prescription Drugs (lifetime)	Hard Drugs (year)
0	83.5%	89.5%	94.7%
1-2	6.0%	4.5%	1.6%
3-9	3.7%	2.3%	1.3%
10-14	2.2%	1.6%	0.8%
20-39	1.5%	0.8%	0.6%
40 or more	3.1%	1.2%	0.9%

Students were asked how many times in the past thirty days had they used marijuana. A large majority of students (83.5%) indicated that they had not used marijuana over the past 30 days, while 6% of students reported using marijuana 1-2 times in that same timeframe. Just over 3% of students reported using marijuana 40 or more times over the past 30 days. Students were also asked how many times in their life they took a prescription drug without a doctor's prescription. The prescription drugs mentioned in the survey included: OxyContin,

Percocet, Vicodin, Ritalin, and Xanax. Nearly 90% of students reported never partaking in illegal prescription drugs, but 4.5% indicated that they did so 1-2 times over the span of their lives. Just over 1% reporting indulging in illegal drugs 40 or more times in the lifetimes. The last drug usage question on the survey asked how many times they used hard drugs in the past year. Nearly 95% of the students reported not using hard drugs over the past year, while almost 2% reported using these drugs between 1 and 9 times over the past year. The final question in the drug section of the survey asked students if anyone had offered, sold, or given them an illegal drug on school property; 16% reported that they had been offered, sold, or given an illegal drug over the past 12 months.

Students were also asked about their participation in risky behaviors during the focus group sessions, but gave a limited number of responses. During a middle school focus group session a female participant reflected on an incident that happened at her old school where there was a girl who was smoking and doing drugs in the 4th grade. This was brought to public light via Facebook and caused the school to check backpacks (afterwards all backpacks had to be clear), personal belongings, and trashcans to find the drugs she was hiding.

A majority of qualitative responses related to risky behaviors came from the open-ended questionnaire given to students after the focus group sessions and reflected students not carrying weapons, drinking alcohol, or taking drugs. However, a high school student indicated that he/she did not "need weapons, but I carry a knife on my key chain." Another high school student reported that they "have carried weapons to school, but not because I was cyberbullied. I carried it just in case anybody wanted to start problems and bring weapons." Whether or not weapons are thought to be used for elements of cyberbullying, they are still ending up in school. Weapons, like those mentioned, could be utilized by students in the event of a physical fight, whether the dispute involved a cyberbullying instance or not. The use of weapons such as these could further escalate an already bad situation.

While students may not perceive a connection between bullying and alcohol or drug use, alcohol or drug use may still be occurring among students in off-school hours. However, some students were aware of what it meant to publicly share pictures of partaking in risky behaviors: "Well some kids have really inappropriate pictures on there and like when they are older, people post drinking pictures and people will get into trouble for that and then a college won't want you." Thus, some students were aware that posting inappropriate comments and pictures referring to drinking and other risky behaviors could potentially affect their future negatively by not allowing them to go to college.

Further Analysis

To further facilitate analysis of the YRBS data to more fully understand the cyberbullying phenomenon, a number of variables were thematically combined to create a set of factors. The *Violence factor* (mean=7.18, median=7.0, standard deviation=2.40) is an aggregate of 4 questions, including questions on frequency of fighting, bringing weapons to school, and perceptions of violence at school. The *Drugs factor* (mean=6.36, median=5.0, standard deviation=3.35) is an aggregate of 8 questions, including questions on the perceived risk of using alcohol and smoking, and the actual usage of: cigarettes, alcohol, marijuana, prescription drugs, and hard drugs (described as cocaine, crack, methamphetamines, ecstasy, or heroin).

Cronbach's alpha coefficients were calculated for each factor to provide a measure of internal consistency. The Violence factor produced a Cronbach's alpha of .446, and the Drugs factor generated a Cronbach's alpha of .591. Factor analysis produced Eigen values, which indicated splitting either of these factors was not appropriate.

To identify the relationships between the risk variables and cyberbullying, a series of ANOVA tests were conducted. Table 12 depicts ANOVA analyses for victimization of cyberbullying.

Table 12: ***ANOVA for Victimization of Cyberbullying***

Risk Variable	F	*p*
Drug Factor	83.744	.000
Violence Factor	47.815	.000
Traditional Bullying	14.797	.000
Age	1.014	.407
Sex	9.183	.000
Race	3.625	.003

A number of these ANOVA findings are significant at the .001 level. Drug usage, participation in school violence (including fighting and bringing weapons to school), and victimization in traditional physical bullying were all highly significant. The demographic variables of sex (where males are more likely to be victims of cyberbullying) and race (where African American students are more likely to be victims of cyberbullying) were also statistically significant. Age, however, was not a statistically significant variable.

Analysis of variance tests were also conducted for the perpetration of cyberbullying. Much like cyberbullying victimization, drug usage, participation in school violence, and traditional bullying victimization were all significant at the .001 level. Table 13 shows the ANOVA analyses for the perpetration of cyberbullying.

Table 13: ***ANOVA for Perpetration of Cyberbullying***

Risk Variable	F	*p*
Drug Factor	86.387	.000
Violence Factor	43.943	.000
Traditional Bullying	10.064	.000
Age	4.377	.001
Sex	10.004	.000
Race	2.747	.018

Race and sex were similarly significant, such that African-American and male students are more likely to commit cyberbullying. Age was statistically significant in that older students are more likely to commit cyberbullying than their younger counterparts.

Finally, analysis of variance tests were conducted for self-reported victimization by traditional bullying. Students were asked whether in the past twelve months they were harassed, picked on, or bullied such that they felt unsafe at school. Table 14 represents the ANOVA analyses for traditional bullying victimization.

Table 14: ***ANOVA for Traditional Bullying Victimization***

Risk Variable	F	*p*
Drug Factor	40.331	.000
Violence Factor	1376.987	.000
Age	40.353	.000
Sex	.832	.362
Race	7.468	.006

Participation in drug usage and school violence (as evidenced by the very large F score) significantly predict traditional bullying victimization. Younger students and non-African-American students are significantly more likely to be victims of traditional bullying.

Regression analyses were conducted to further specify the relationship between the independent and dependent variables.

Regression Analyses

Ordinary least squares models were assembled to identify variance explained when a set of dependent variables were regressed on the independent variables of cyberbullying victimization, cyberbullying perpetration, and traditional bullying victimization. Table 15 describes the results of those models.

Table 15: *Estimates from Regression Analyses*

Dependent Variable	R	R^2	F	*p*
Cyberbullying Victimization[a]	.307	.109	77.12	.000
Cyberbullying Perpetration[b]	.323	.105	73.14	.000
Traditional Bullying Victimization[c]	.559	.312	364.06	.000

a. Model Predictors: (Constant), Traditional Bullying, Drug Factor, Violence Factor, Sex, Age

b. Model Predictors: (Constant), Traditional Bullying, Drug Factor, Violence Factor, Sex, Age

c. Model Predictors: (Constant), Drug Factor, Violence Factor, Sex, Age

Regression analyses indicate that each of the specified models were statistically significant at the .001 level. Although the R^2 values for the cyberbullying victimization and cyberbullying perpetration models are not large, they are highly significant. Given the large N of over 3,400 subjects, these significant outcomes are meaningful. A review of the standardized Beta scores produced findings consistent with the ANOVA outcomes.

Students spoke at length about different aspects of cyberbullying. It was something that they were aware of and if they, themselves, had not been involved in a cyberbullying incident they knew of someone that had been. From the speed of information transmission to how it affects victims, students shared their thoughts and experiences regarding this phenomenon.

It was evident that students utilize social technology tools frequently and on an ongoing basis to stay in touch with their fellow students. One student commented that they "used Facebook because almost everybody finds out what happened by using the Internet." The way information is shared among teenagers has been transformed. Instead of students just able to chat about what happened that day when they were face-to-face or when their parents let them use the family's landline phone, they can now be shared in an instant through personal cell phones, social network sites, and other Internet tools. Students were quick to point out how quickly information spreads via social technology tools. A male high school student said that once any kind of information is "on Facebook, or any type of Internet it just blows up…because Internet's everywhere no matter where you are at." He later added:

> Exactly, you can tell somebody here and then they tell somebody in Greendale or somebody in Sheboygan they tell someone in Racine, then Chicago knows about it and then it's going to spread over the whole United States. Next thing you know somebody in Florida is talking about you.

Information not only spreads quickly, but can do so over vast amounts of geographical space. Due to the nature of networked relationships something embarrassing or gossip can happen at school, be posted on someone's Facebook wall, and seen by all their friends whether they go to that school or another school in the city, state, country, or world. This is quite different from rumors and gossip that used to be contained to a few cliques of friends. Now information is available to their whole "friend" network. While students indicated that most of their friends on Facebook were from their school or general vicinity and were connected through school-based activities (e.g., sports), others indicated that they had cousins their age and friends from other parts of the state, United States, and Mexico.

Some students were conscious of the reach of social network relationships, as well the permanence associated with the act of posting messages. A female middle school student said that she was careful about what she posts "because everyone can see it and it will never go away." However, not all students realized that the things they post on Facebook or send via text can be shared with many others instantly in a way that can never be taken back.

Students were clear about how often teenagers utilized social network sites. They also spoke about the overlap between school and social network sites that often created a space for cyberbullying activity that extends from school to the social network environment and to school again, as well as *vice versa*. The high school students spoke especially poignantly to this idea. During the focus group session a female participant said that "Facebook is where everything happens." A male student indicated that when a fight happens at school "the first thing they do they go on Facebook and they say no names but everybody knows who they are talkin' about... that's how things get started."

With social network sites such as Facebook being utilized by a majority of the student body, students that get into an altercation during school take it to the social network site after the school day. The reverse is true, as well, as inter-personal altercations can begin in cyberspace and end up in the school environment. A female student spoke to this by saying that people start things on "Facebook, but they can't leave it alone and it comes back to school and gets started all over again." Middle school students also commented on the overlap between the social network and face-to-face environments. A female student talked about how if a person is "writing on their wall they are made fun of in school" too. In a different middle school focus group session, students were asked to comment on the observation that the same people that bully others in person also cyberbully people online. A female student reported in this regard: "It could be different but...I think they take it a step further on Facebook, but they are basically the same people."

Students spoke at length about the role that rumors and gossip played in their own lives, a topic which was discussed in an earlier section. However, students indicated that when rumors and gossip occurred they usually did not stop during the confines of the school day. The connection between bullying, gossip, and rumors in person and online was mentioned by many study participants. Students that are bullied in person may also be cyberbullied on social network sites. Likewise, the perpetrators are likely to be some of the same individuals or groups of individuals as they share information in person that they also would post about a victim on a social network site.

CHAPTER SUMMARY

Students are being bullied to the point where many of them feel unsafe at school and some are missing school because they perceive the school setting to be unsafe. A small number of students reported bringing weapons to school, potentially exacerbating dangerous settings. While fighting was not common, around 30% of students reported participating in a physical fight on school grounds over the span of the previous twelve months.

Both cyberbullying victims and perpetrators share a number of co-existing variables, including drug usage (such as marijuana, prescription drugs, or hard drugs), engagement with violence (such as fighting or bringing weapons to school), and engagement in traditional bullying. Victims of traditional bullying are also more likely to engage in drug use and violent behavior. Males are more likely to engage in cyberbullying activity (as both perpetrator and victim). Survey results showed that older students are more likely to commit acts of cyberbullying on younger students. Inferential analyses were consistent with one another, suggesting that drug use and violent behaviors are predictors of cyberbullying victimization, cyberbullying perpetration, and traditional bullying victimization alike.

During focus group sessions students were quite clear that cyberbullying was happening and that social technology tools were effecting the speed at which information was spread to others in their school, city, state, and country. A consistent theme across all four focus group sessions was the topic of gossip and rumors among peers, both online and at school. The following chapter will document the role gossip and rumors plays in the lives of teenagers in this study.

CHAPTER 5

Gossip and Rumors: Same Story, Different Day

> "This is like gossip central here. There's so many students here and not just so many students here but everybody knows everybody so if the gossip gets into the wrong hands, it is automatically mutilated, twisted around."— Male high school student

Gossip and rumors in middle and high school are nothing new. In fact, this has been common among youth for decades. Gossip and rumors were the focal point of communication when we were in high school, and probably were for our parents as well. While the person at the focal point of the gossip and rumors may change, the nature and topics endure. Although the topics under discussion have not evolved, the rate at which gossip and rumors can spread through the latest social technology has changed dramatically.

GOSSIP AND RUMORS

In our focus groups with students, gossip and rumors dominated every conversation with students sharing who typically spreads the news, when it gets spread, and how gossip and rumors work. The section will close with what the gossip and rumors are typically about, how people react to gossip and rumors, who people put their trust in regarding such news, and the overlap between Facebook and the school environment.

Not Random or Specifically Timed

Students indicated that gossip was something that happened with people you know rather than among random people to whom they would not normally talk. A male high school focus group participant characterized the spread of gossip in this manner:

> …you don't just go to random people and they are going to tell you the gossip about something. You have to know who

> you are talking to in order to find the gossip. I wouldn't go to "Max" to tell him—it wouldn't make sense. Gossip that you don't know nothing about, it wouldn't be fun.

Therefore, gossip is information about people that you know and is something that gets spread through mutual friends and acquaintances. In the school environment individuals who do not know each other do not interact just to spread gossip. Instead, an existing relationship and a mutual interest in the gossip must have been previously established. This male high school student—like others that participated in the focus group sessions—also accorded importance to gossip indicating that he actively sought out the gossip and felt that it was fun. In a follow-up question regarding where (e.g., home, school, etc.) he typically heard gossip, he replied "Anytime—at the moment." With the increasing use of social technology such as texting and social network usage it further increases the speed and reach of the gossip. Instead of gossip just being spread during school hours or through a few friends at night by landline telephone, which used to be at least somewhat monitored by parents, students now have access to their peer groups 24/7. This continuous accessibility allows gossip to reach more people very quickly.

It's Like the Telephone Game...

The nature of gossip and rumors is that they spread quickly and to a lot of people. One student described it as once "one person knows it . . . then everybody knows it." While students indicated that gossip only occurred between individuals that knew one another, they also spoke of their school's interconnectedness:

> **Male High School Focus Group Participant:** This is like gossip central here. There's so many students here and not just so many students here but everybody knows everybody so if the gossip gets into the wrong hands, it is automatically mutilated, twisted around.

In a smaller school most students are connected in some way—through classes, through sports, or through mutual friends. Even though students had indicated that you just do not go up to anyone to talk about gossip, there are connections between groups of students and mutual interests that spur the cycle of spreading rumors and gossip. This student also mentioned that information gets mutilated and twisted around as it moves through different people and various groups of people. A female middle school student commented that "it might start out as something that's like not a big deal and then other people transform it into something that's a lot worse than it was in the first place." During most of the focus group sessions students likened the twisted information that involved in gossip and rumors to the telephone game:

> **Female High School Focus Group Participant:** It's almost like playing telephone—I tell someone something, he puts it into his own words and he's going to tell it so a lot things get mixed up.

> **Male High School Focus Group Participant:** Like the game telephone... like when you just say something and you pass it down the line and then the person at the end says it, says what they heard and the person at the beginning says what they said. Then you see if it became different, so how people change it.

Gossip and rumors are like the game telephone in that they both start with a statement that can turn into something very different by the end. Students also offered some examples of what gossip and rumors usually involve.

What's the Good Word?

When asked what gossip and rumors were typically about, students reported a range of possibilities. A common theme to gossip and rumors was a focus on relationships with a potential romantic partner. A male high school focus group participant said they focus on "Who somebody been with. Or what somebody did with somebody else over the weekend. Post it on Facebook." Another male high school focus group participant shared his recent experience of being the center of the gossip:

> False truths or even if it is the truth you don't want it to be out there. Kind of like this happened to me—in the beginning of

> the school year where I was with this girl and first we were just friends talking. And then out of nowhere somebody told—I don't know how but I found out even—the girls mom that I was hanging out with found out that we were supposedly having sex in school. I was like 'Whoa, I barely gave her a hug today.' That's what I'm saying.

This young man described rumors and gossip as either something a person does not want out in the open or something that was a complete fabrication. Together, these young men bring up an important aspect regarding peer interaction and gossip—that it often tended to focus on sexuality in the form of whom people are dating and how their relationship is advancing.

During the focus group sessions female participants spoke of how jealousy often creates gossip and rumors among female friend groups. One female high school student said:

> It's like sometimes Freshmen they sit there and talk about a person. Like most of the times with the girls it will be like jealousy. That's one of the main things. It's jealousy they just they don't like seeing girls with more stuff than they got. They just talk. Like somebody talked about my sister and there was a group of Freshmen that were talking she got some money or whatever and she got some new shoes. It's like why wouldn't she it's her money. They just childish.

This student points to age and gender playing a role in gossip and rumors. Older students tended to believe that the younger students (e.g., Freshmen) played a large part in gossip and rumors as they lacked maturity. In this case this student indicated that these young female students were unsure of how to deal with their feelings regarding not having money for material items and it manifested itself in gossip.

A male middle school focus group participant also shared an altercation that happened between female students: "One time this year there was a girl in a fight...based on physical appearance." This student indicated that gossip and rumors can sometimes lead to verbal and physical fights. He also pointed out another aspect that gossip and rumors focus on: physical appearance. As teenagers come of age they may pick on others based on their own insecurities. According to another male middle school student, sometimes there seems to be no reason at all for picking on others and starting rumors:

> Sometimes people just say mean things. Like for no reason at all, they say to be mean. I saw once—this on one of my friend's statuses—he said why can't anybody hang out and then one person commented because no one likes you. Just said it to be mean.

An aspect of this might also be the medium. When people are in person they have the opportunity to read body language, see facial expressions, and hear tone of voice to determine what the other person means. Through things like Facebook and texting individuals do not have that luxury, and at times things that were meant to be taken in a joking manner come off as being mean. Lack of seeing someone face-to-face may also allow people to say things they would not say in person.

During a time when teenagers are coming of age aspects they deem important within their peer culture manifest themselves in rumors and gossip. These things include, but are not limited to: sexual attraction and relationships, material possessions and jealousy, and physical appearances. However, rumors and gossip are not limited to these aspects or aspects related to them, and students tended to have very different reactions to gossip.

Reactions to Gossip

Students explained that there were many different reactions possible to gossip. One male high school student spoke of how both little things and big things can hurt gossip victims:

> Like even the littlest thing can hurt someone. If it's something huge it can harm them a lot but if it's something little over time it will build up and keep coming back at you and you are still going to feel bad.

Something huge, like the rumor about the young man having sex with his friend when they had not, can be embarrassing and hurtful to the individuals involved in the rumor. However, small rumors and little pieces of gossip (e.g., that someone has money) can build up and affect someone just as much as a larger rumor or piece of gossip can.

Students also commented about the people that tend to participate in circulating rumors. A male high school student talked about how people often act without thinking:

> Like a rumor or something spreads the person is going to automatically react to this or I heard you saying that. I think they act out of anger before they actually stop and think why it's being said and if they actually know if it's true or not.

When people hear a rumor they sometimes react without thinking about who may have started the rumor, why they started it, and how much of it may or may not be true. A female high school student reported that some students are prone to spreading rumors as a deflecting mechanism: "I just think people have egos and trying to protect their egos. When a rumor comes around they are trying to protect themselves." If a rumor is circulating about someone else, you are less likely to be a victim of a rumor that day. Thus, spreading it becomes a way to protect yourself as well as a way to pump up your ego as you are not the one being picked on.

A male high school student thought that rumors were more prevalent among younger students than among upper classmen:

> …most of the rumors start off with Freshmans. I analyzed this, they all start with the Freshmen then they go spreading that thing. When you come to the upper classman I guess they build some maturity or they realize how much [name of school] is and that's how the rumors are that's how I would react. I would go straight to the person hey, you were talking about that stuff what is that?

This student believed that upper classmen typically had more maturity and were more likely to go to people if they thought they were spreading rumors about them instead of adding to the spreading of the rumors or participating in an escalation (e.g., fight). Some students indicated that they did not participate in rumors or gossip at all. A male high school student focused on believing things he saw over what he heard from others: "I was raised to think that gossip is as fake as the person who told you. I believe in depending on what I saw." In the case of this young man, he was taught by his parent(s) or guardian(s) to not believe gossip because it was likely to be untrue and to instead trust only what he saw. A female high school student talked about how she wished that if people had problems with other people, they would talk to them instead of starting rumors:

> I like to say that if you have problems with somebody just go to that person and talk to them. Sometimes they talk about me like why she always dressed like that. I'm here why don't you just come to me and ask me a question like why are you wearing this or why do you do what you do. That's why there are problems…they just think about themselves. If I had this problem I would want them to come to me…They think it's cool to talk about other people and make fun of other people…I'll be looking at them and I'm like OK, I am going to ignore you.

As this student pointed out, it would be best when a student had a problem with another student to talk it out instead of talking behind their back and spreading rumors. However, many students commented that confronting people for such conversations is rare. It turns out, then, that spreading rumors and gossip can make some teenagers feel powerful, feel better about themselves, and be a source of entertainment. Given these observations, this student suggests that it is just best to ignore people who are inclined to spread rumors.

Whom to Trust?

Many students commented that it was important to know whom to trust with your secrets and information you did not want shared with others. A female middle school student explained that sometimes people "like talking about what happened with them during the day" and "maybe they don't want this other person to know." When they talk about what happened to them they leave the power in the hands of the person they told to keep it quiet. Students further indicated that often individuals put their trust in the wrong people. A female high school student shared her thoughts in this regard, noting the following:

> …you know you can't tell everybody your personal business. When I come to school every day I see a lot of people doing that—whatever they did with their friend, their boyfriend and

> they come to the friend...and basically it's going to go round school you know.

When things happen in life people sometimes like to share these things with their friends. However, this is not always wise because it can start the dreaded chain of gossip. This student advocated for a discretionary approach where if you do not want things going around about you to keep your personal business largely to yourself. Once other teenagers know things about another teenager they can sometimes be relentless with spreading gossip and keeping it in mainstream conversation. A female high school student shared her thoughts on this issue, noting the following:

> ...sometimes people just don't know when to stop talking. It could hurt somebody if it come back to them because the person they told they thought wouldn't say anything, they find everybody in the school knows.

This student brings up many pertinent points about gossip among teenagers. First, sometimes teenagers do not know their limits and the limits of their peers. At times they might not know when to stop gossiping, and do not have a full understanding of the difference between joking and bullying. Further, they do not always see the impact of their actions. By spreading gossip and rumors they could really hurt someone unknowingly. One female high school student said that she did not trust many people at school because they were fake:

> Here you meet a lot of fake people. The people I meet like sometimes try to be your friend and when you turn around they trying to laugh at you making fun of who you are and stuff. I've seen a lot of stuff going on here. I look at people sometimes—I don't hang out with a lot of people, a lot of people don't know me. I look at people to know who they are because I am who I am and I'm proud of myself being who I am but some people don't' realize who they are and they keep making fun of people who are being themselves.

She said that she stayed away from a lot of people because they were just interested in being popular and spreading rumors to make themselves feel better. She also thought that teenagers that make fun of others do not have an understanding of who they are and are jealous of others who might be happy with who they are.

Exacerbated by Social Technologies

One important way gossip and rumors differ from when I was in school was how gossip and rumors are affected by social technologies. Participants in the student focus group sessions indicated that, for the most part, rumors and gossip started many fights on Facebook. A female middle school student said that someone "started a rumor I was going to fight another chick and I did not even know her." In the end, the other girl really wanted to fight her and they ended up in a physical fight. A male high school student described that due to cell phones that have texting and Internet capabilities students get gossip, rumors, and the latest news about their peers quickly:

> Even like, for example, like if we are at school and like a fight breaks out. Everybody knows about it even though they are not physically there talking to someone that knows what happened it goes around somehow. And people end up knowing not even by the end of the first period then. That's how fast it spreads.

Gossip, rumors, and the latest news about peers are exacerbated by social technologies such as Facebook and texting. A male high school student shared an experience where Facebook and texting played different roles in an actual physical fight that occurred after a talent show. He said that a fight broke out after some students that did not go to their school attended their talent show (but were friends with students at his school) and were offended at how a few students at his school were dancing and felt like they were trying to show off. These visitors posted comments to Facebook about this, and others began to pile on posting things like they would "whoop him" or "jump him." Facebook posts and in-person making fun of people who had danced at the talent show, made for a large commotion. The young man who told the story left before the fight broke out, but received texts about how he should come back and how there was a fight going down. While social technologies give teenagers the opportunity to explore their identity and interests, it also provides a space for students—even from different schools—to start drama. Students now are even more connected to other local schools than they used to be. Students who leave a school or go to a different middle or high school than their friends can still keep connected through things such as Facebook.

In middle school some female focus group participants said that "boy drama" seemed to cause a lot of problems, both on Facebook and in person. They explained as follows:

> **Female Focus Group Participant 1:** Well there is, we have a friend, she usually has boy drama. She posts it on Facebook and like you are a fake friend or whatever, stuff like that. But she doesn't mention any names.
>
> **Female Focus Group Participant 2:** But people know when you are talking about them. It's obvious.
>
> **Female Focus Group Participant 1:** Because something that is said in school she put on Facebook and people start commenting on it.

Facebook can further intensify something that happened at school, when in the past it may have fizzled away with time from the situation. Like these students shared, something that happens at school can be posted on Facebook and the issue gets magnified by other people commenting on the situation. Even if names of others involved are not posted, students still have an understanding of to whom the Facebook posting refers as they know what happened at school that day.

Rumors and gossip in middle school seemed to revolve around boys (for girls) and girls (for boys). One girl said that another girl posted that a boy was cute on Facebook, and another girl said, "too bad that boy is mine" and a bunch of other people got involved and "called each other not so nice names." One female middle school participant gave an example from her old school where two boys were friends. One of them liked this girl and he was ready to tell her how he felt when his friend said he liked her. They argued over the issue online, and one ended up punching the other.

Many students made a point to comment on how things that start on Facebook end up at school. Middle school participants indicated that rumors can start in school, and then proliferate on social network sites.

The converse can also happen as rumors and arguments start online then materialize in school in face-to-face altercations—either physical or verbal. A female middle school participant said that sometimes people "post things that they think won't cause problem but they come to school and it causes drama." This student brought up an important point in that sometimes people do not have foresight and do not have a comprehensive understanding of their peers to know how different comments will affect them. A male middle school student talked about how whether people hear a piece of news on Facebook or in person they are bound to hear it:

> Things can get brought back to school [from Facebook]…that's how you guys know each other...so it's oh, that person did this and that and it gets back to the principal or someone like a teacher. Yeah, it gets back to school and everyone hears about it.

There is a reciprocal relationship between Facebook and in-school forms of communication as it relates to gossip, rumors, and peer news. Between seeing their peers for a large chunk of every weekday of the school year and having access to these same individuals after school and on weekends, social technologies are changing the way inter-peer communication is taking place among teenagers. This constant access to communication gives students the opportunity to maintain closeness with their friends—to feel needed and loved—but it also provides ample space for rumors, gossip, and cyberbullying activity. An interesting aspect, that students seemed unsure about, was at what point does a rumor or a piece of gossip about someone become bullying or cyberbullying.

CHAPTER SUMMARY

This chapter depicts an interesting, albeit enduring, phenomenon of rumors and gossip among middle and high school youth. Students revealed that rumors and gossip played a large role in their lives. They likened rumors and gossip to the "telephone game" and reported that they focused on things like sexual attraction and relationships, material possessions and jealousy, and physical appearances. They also indicated that it was important to react in the right manner and to put your trust in the right people. Further, gossip and rumors can be advanced by speed and to larger audiences with the use of social technologies like Facebook.

CHAPTER 6

Understanding the Cyberbullying Phenomenon

> "Facebook is kind of a whole different world compared to like meeting your friends in person. So, people say stuff they wouldn't normally and then you get to school the next day, it's awkward." —Female middle school student

Key elements of the student focus group sessions included gaining an understanding of how students defined cyberbullying, how cyberbullying occurs, and the factors that contribute to cyberbullying behavior. The following subsections of this chapter document student insights related to these areas.

DEFINING CYBERBULLYING

When students were asked how they would define cyberbullying, they often started off with quite basic definitions. A female middle school student indicated that cyberbullying happened when "you are bullied through the Internet." Another female middle school student in a different focus group session added that cyberbullying occurred when someone "abuses the Internet to hurt another person." To further elaborate on this definition, another female in the focus group session added that it often took the form of blackmailing (i.e., letting information out about people they do not want known to everyone) or going home and updating their Facebook status saying this person is a "B" [participant indicated that she meant an expletive] and that they go back and forth with comments that keep the fight going. A male middle school focus group participant in a different session also commented that this was a common form of cyberbullying. He reported that cyberbullying happens when "you say negative and then everyone comments on that."

Students also indicated that cyberbullying was similar to bullying that occurred in person, but that there were noteworthy differences as well. A male high school student spoke to this as follows:

> It's just basically like the regular social bullying done through the Internet. The only reason I think that affects people more is because it's anger through what they say, but the fact that they are being so fake doing it behind a screen and going behind others backs. Like not even having the courage to be there just irritates me. If somebody wants to say something—even if it's not about me—I'm ready to go off for that and you're fake.

While cyberbullying has many of the same components (e.g., spreading gossip or rumors) and feel (e.g., anger, hurt, etc.) as face-to-face bullying, one difference mentioned by students was the faceless component associated with being online. As reflected in the student's comment cited above and many other comments made by other focus group participants, cyberbullying was seen as a cowardly way of dealing with a problem with another student. Being at home, alone, and behind a computer screen gives some individuals courage or an aloofness to say things that they normally would not say in front a person in fear of a face-to-face repercussion (e.g., fight or verbal confrontation), unpopularity, or loss of friends. This also speaks to group norms and physical cues. In the content of an open-ended questionnaire entry a middle school student wrote:

> …it was a fight between my friends and I didn't know what was going to happen. When I got to school I was talking to her and she understood me. After that everything came back to normal.

Without seeing how another person may be reacting to you, you may be left unsure of how far is too far and what is really happening.

A female high school student spoke about how Facebook allows people to post anything and how cyberbullying starts:

> It's like Facebook is so open you can post anything on there and it's like certain people do certain stuff and if somebody wants to find out something they go onto somebody's site and then put two and two together. That just starts something or they can just…send somebody a picture and that can start something. It's various things that start arguments or teasing

> or whatever. Some people...don't get offended because they got self-esteem. I know I'm not going to worry about this or that but other people are sensitive.

This student brought up an important aspect in that individuals often upload items to their Facebook accounts such as pictures and status messages updating what they are doing. These messages sometimes provoke reaction from others and give clues to other students that actually enable gossip and rumors that start things like fights and teasing. Once fighting and teasing emerges it depends on the individual as to how the situation progresses. If students are sensitive or have relatively low self-esteem, they are more likely to be bothered by the situation and engage in retaliation behavior whereas those with higher self-esteem are not going to let it worry them excessively.

Focus group participants made it clear that cyberbullying did not always appear as bullying. A male high school focus group participant said that:

> It doesn't even have to be bullying or rumors it could be simple—a person that by looking they call them by a name they don't like it. It's started by little things, name-calling and it progresses to rumors.

This student made it clear that progression is often an aspect of cyberbullying. It can start by a student looking at another student in the hallway the wrong way, and that student calling them a name. Then, not liking being called that name that student might start a rumor about the other student. This rumor could manifest between people at school and be spread through texts and online via Facebook. A male high school student added that sometimes this progression can even happen between friends:

> It could happen to anybody—even between two friends you know...like teasing ...and it would be OK because we would be having fun but then I try doing it to somebody else or they get offended by you or my friend gets offended, basically when it goes too far that's when it gets to escalate.

According to this student, the progression to cyberbullying from minor points of tension can happen at anytime. This can even occur in the case of two friends joking around—especially if one of the friends takes offense during the exchange. This can be particularly fluid as different things happen to individuals everyday that could change their outlook on joking around exchanges. What might be all in fun one day might mean something very different to an individual on a day where their parents yelled at them in the morning and they did poorly on a History exam, for example. However, a female middle school student indicated that "if you are really close to them and know them you might understand why they are acting that way and if they are not really you get mad back at them, you get annoyed." If a friend lashes out, you might have insight into why they may say mean things to you or react in a hurt manner toward something you joke about often. Having this insight allows friends to cut each other slack. However, with students that are not close friends or to friends unwilling to share things this understanding is not present, and their absence may provide space for annoyance that can provide an ignition for cyberbullying and bullying activity.

Students did reveal some problematic aspects to defining cyberbullying. A male high school student said that they "don't use the word cyberbullying... we'll be like people talking [smack]." Cyberbullying is not a term that students seem to use and view it as the adult word for gossip, rumors, and "smack" that takes place on the Internet. Interestingly enough, students seem not to separate cyberbullying from bullying, gossip, rumors, and smack. Instead, they all mingle together under a large entity that the students did not name. This reveals a difference in conceptualization between academia and practice that needs to be bridged. It also leads to students being unsure of what cyberbullying actually is. A male high school student indicated in this regard:

> Cyberbullying...it's such a loose term...they don't realize what cyberbullying is till it's happening to them that's why you see some people on Facebook who argue and go back and forth because they don't know what they're doing or if it's cyberbullying or if it's bullying at all. They are not aware of it because they haven't been in that type of environment for too long or just being given a broad knowledge of what's going on

> like how we are discussing cyberbullying right now, they are alienated from that.

With students unsure of what cyberbullying actually is, they may be engaging in the objectionable behavior without knowing they are doing so. Without further educational opportunities that allow students to become more acclimated to what cyberbullying encompasses they may continue to unknowingly engage in cyberbullying activity that harms not only others, but may harm themselves.

HOW DOES CYBERBULLYING HAPPEN?

As students that took part in the focus group sessions they shared the common ways that cyberbullying tended to take place. One way students mentioned was through social network status messages:

> **Female Middle School Focus Group Participant:** A lot of people talk about people in their statuses like you should just lay off because you are blah-blah just like say all this stuff and don't put their name and also. You don't need to share that on Facebook you can keep that to yourself because that's how people start fighting about that kind of stuff that doesn't need to be put out.
>
> **Male Middle School Focus Group Participant:** Then like you ask who said that about me and oh text me something like that well they can't say it.
>
> **Focus Group Moderator:** Do other people know who it's about really?
>
> **Female Middle School Focus Group Participant:** Yeah, sometimes.

Social network status messages provide space for cyberbullying activity as it allows individuals to update their status, vent, and talk about other people to a large audience without having to include their name; this anonymity provides a level of safety. For the most part, because many people know what had happened during the school day, individuals know about whom people are talking even without including the person's name. When they do not know who the person is posting about and ask on the thread, the original poster typically says that they cannot say it to the larger audience and to text them if they wanted to know who they were talking about. This points to an interesting intersection of the use of multiple tools in cyberbullying activity. In this case it was the use of a social network status message and texting. In an open-ended questionnaire entry a middle school student shared a cyberbullying experience that included texting, an instant messenger, and a social network site:

> It all started because of a text. That text was sent to one of my friends. That text was saying that I was saying mean things about my friend that weren't true. Then my friend sent me a nasty IM and I was like okay? My friend who was with me told me to update my [social network] status and I did. Then that girl started commiting [sic] on it and a fight started. Then that person who sent the text said it was a joke. I was actually mad because I didn't know what was going on.

When using multiple tools in cyberbullying activity the initial victim may in turn become a perpetrator when defending themselves. This works to create a reciprocal nature to some cyberbullying activity. In this student's example a friend sent him/her a text message saying that he/she was spreading rumors about a common friend. Then the friend started sending him/her mean instant messages. At this point the victim was convinced by another friend to update his/her social network status message to reflect the situation that was occurring. With that status message in the general public the person about whom the victim had been accused of spreading rumors started commenting on the thread and online fighting occurred. All this was a misunderstanding, as the person who had sent the original text was just trying to cause drama.

A cyberbullying situation does not have to be limited to a victim and a perpetrator. Sometimes the line becomes more difficult to determine as the reciprocal nature can emerge and a victim can defend him/herself, making them a perpetrator as well. Also, situations can be quite complex. When you include social technologies in a bullying action, it becomes much more open to other individuals, a fact which further creates the potential for more perpetrators, victims, and witnesses.

Status messages were just one way students reported cyberbullying taking place on social network sites. A female middle school student said: "in different schools I've been in, some girls posted stuff on another girl's wall and they actually were big fights." Another female middle school student added that when students are cyberbullying through the wall function "they are made fun of in school." The wall function on social network sites also provides space where cyberbullying can take place by posting messages about another person. Cyberbullying perpetrators can post messages on the victim's wall or can post something about the victim on their own wall, which the victim does not have the power to delete. These students point out an important aspect of cyberbullying in that it does not confine itself to just the abstract space of being online. Instead, it often crosses over into their school lives as their network of "friends" frequently overlaps.

Another way individuals can be cyberbullied via social network is through multi-media facets incorporated into these sites. A female middle school student spoke about how pictures can be problematic:

> …people can post stuff that happens. You get tagged or someone posts a picture of you. Something like that can be really embarrassing and they don't delete it and get into like a fight kind of thing over that because they don't delete it and it can really embarrass someone.

Members of social network sites can take pictures with their mobile devices or digital cameras and upload them to the site without the permission of those individuals who may appear in the pictures. This becomes a problem when a picture of someone that they might find embarrassing cannot be removed until the original poster removes it. This cyberbullying act can leave the victim feeling defenseless as the picture of them stays in cyberspace without their control. Individuals can also tag—or associate a name—with someone in a picture so that it appears on that person's wall. With advancements in mobile technologies many students now have mobile phones that can record video clips. A female focus group participant got into an argument with a guy who had recorded her friend in an altercation at a soccer game. He posted it to YouTube and eventually to Facebook where other people made comments making fun of the participant's friend, commenting that her friend fared poorly in the fight. People "liked" these comments and it escalated to threats of fighting. However, video clips are not limited to capturing an event in progress and commenting on it later among a large audience. In an open-ended questionnaire entry a high school student wrote about the cyberbullying videos she had seen on Facebook:

> Some kids made a video and posted it on Facebook talking about how these kids are saying this girl engages in sexual activity and talking about how these kids dress.

Instead of just using words through text, perpetrators can use video and pictures as another venue to spread rumors, gossip, and make fun of others.

Social network sites also have a group function that allows people to create groups anonymously. Individuals can be added to the group without even knowing they have been added. Cyberbullying perpetrators can use this group function as a venue to victimize other students. A male middle school student shared his experience during a focus group session:

> There is this one kid who, he made a group that was called "Meggie" and it was this name that people always said for this girl named Megan and then they would always say Meggie and she didn't like it and she told them to stop. On Facebook you can add people to your groups, there's no way of knowing if you get added to this group, so I got called down to the office because I was in this group and I didn't even know that I was in it—somebody added me to the group. So I got in trouble for that…I had to leave the group and the person who created the group had to delete it and then I had to talk to Megan's parents about why I was in the group and I said I didn't know I was in it and I was added into it.

The Facebook groups function, which was created to allow groups of individuals to interact without having to post on walls or in private messages, can be used by students looking to cyberbully another student. Groups can be formulated anonymously—without being able to identify who started it—and can be a space where students can gather to make fun or spread rumors about a fellow student. In the case of this student he indicated that he did not even know he was in the group until he got into trouble for being part of it.

On social network sites individuals can also create other identities with the specific purpose of bullying others, a fact which gives them a cloak of anonymity. A male middle school student cited this as an example: "There was this one guy, like I don't know, but he's like 24/25 on Facebook and his name is Uglies…he like grades people on how bad they look and stuff." When middle and high school students friend an anonymous source like this it can be a source of entertainment to watch this individual make fun of others. However, it can leave those that are made fun of feeling bad about themselves and how they look.

Students commented that this anonymity was a main difference between bullying and cyberbullying. A middle school female said that this can be unnerving because "you don't know who that person might be sometimes." A high school student, in their open-ended questionnaire entry, indicated that there was a sense of helplessness associated with anonymous cyberbullying because "a lot of times the pages/person is anonymous so there isn't really anything you can say about it!" When asked if cyberbullying was the same as bullying, middle school focus group participants said:

> **Female Middle School Student 1:** Same thing, more strong.
>
> **Female Middle School Student 2:** Cyberbullying it can get more out of hand because you are not face-to-face you could say whatever.

Cyberbullying can be perceived as being more strong and impactful towards victims as it is exacerbated by the lack of being face-to-face with others. Students thought that cyberbullying was stronger because before the Internet people could get away from bullying, as it was usually restricted to school. However, with the Internet as a major component, cyberbullying can go on all day creating a bad cycle. A common observation by many students was that the reason cyberbullying was worse and had more potential to spiral out of control was that the people that are involved are not in the same physical space. Middle school focus group participants spoke about this:

> **Female Focus Group Participant:** If you were there in person there'd be no way you would say any of this stuff to anyone's face, but yet they write it on their status. Things like stuff that they would never say to you personally and then it gets into this big thing.

> **Male Focus Group Participant:** Because they think nobody else will know.

These students thought that students often said things that they would never say in person. They thought that it could be due to the anonymous component (e.g., by not directly writing the name of the person they are referencing in a status message), which gives them courage to say things when they normally would not in person. By masking who they are talking about students sometimes have an unrealistic expectation that only the people they want to know will know what and who they are referencing. Another middle school student shared her thoughts on this:

> **Female Focus Group Participant:** And then Facebook is kind of a whole different world compared to like meeting your friends in person. So, people say stuff they wouldn't normally and then you get to school the next day, it's awkward.

This student described Facebook as a whole different world. It can certainly feel like that to students, as a perceived anonymity can feel like a protection that gives them courage to say things they normally would not. The lack of physical cues from other students with whom they interact can also give them an uncertainty if they went too far, creating an awkward feeling waiting to see how their next face-to-face interaction will go.

Factors Contributing to Cyberbullying Involvement

Students cited many factors that contributed to cyberbullying involvement. Focus group participants indicated that, for the most part, rumors and gossip started fights. Rumors and gossip seemed to revolve around boys (for girls) and girls (for boys). When asked what often starts fights online two, female middle school students described the following:

> **Focus Group Participant 1:** Boys.
>
> **Focus Group Participant 2:** Usually hear of fights about boys. It's annoying but we hear about it because it's a small school.

A female focus group participant in another session said that one girl posted that a boy was cute on Facebook and another girl said, "too bad that boy is mine." Then a bunch of other people got involved and "called each other not so nice names." A different female middle school student shared an experience where she went to a party with her boyfriend and her boyfriend took a picture of them, which he posted to Facebook. A friend of his, who was a girl, posted mean things like "you look good, but she doesn't." The female focus group participant told her to back off and the other girl kept calling her names. A female high school student shared an example of how a guy she liked caused a cyberbullying act to take place:

> I guess me and a couple of girls like the same guy. And he liked me. So they started trying to put me down, talking about me, teasing me, trying to make their selves feel better.

In these cases females fight over boys and utilize social network sites to pick on their competition. The female high school student did provide perspective as to why this happened. When individuals like the same person they put down their competition because they feel threatened. Feeling threatened makes them want to make themselves look and feel better. A way to do this is to post comments on Facebook degrading the other(s) involved and to have other students comment in support—in essence, taking their side.

While most of the examples about rumors and gossip related to individuals liking one another were mostly centered around females, a female middle school focus group participant did give an example from her old school where two boys were friends and one of them liked this girl. He was ready to tell her how he felt when his friend said he liked her. They argued online and one ended up punching the other. Cyberbullying related to jealousy did not just occur between individuals vying for the attention of someone in whom they were interested; it also occurred between friends in the same friend group. A female middle school student told a story from her old school where a girl was mad at her because during a dance more girls hung out with her. The girl that was mad posted a status message on MySpace about the dance and comments were posted in response. Students continually cited face-to-face incidents revolving around rumors and gossip that they ended up fighting about over a social network site. With students reporting up to 4,000 "friends" and typically friending those they go to school with, it is very easy for fights to go viral with students who are not even in the fight choosing sides and coming to the rescue of their "friend."

The most common factors related to cyberbullying were rumors and gossip around meaningful relationships with others. Related to this, students cited rumors and gossip around sexuality and promiscuity as also starting cyberbullying in the past. A female middle school student said that at her old school there were two boys who were cousins in the same class. Other kids were scared to tell on them when they did bad things. There was a party on a Friday night and one boy who was gay was hanging out with the boys and the cousins thought he was doing it to get close to boys in a sexual way (since he usually hung out with girls). The cousins went home after the party and posted things on Facebook about the boy being gay that were mean and the boy's friends, who were girls, came to his defense. The online fighting continued as the cousins said the boy was a wimp for having girls stand up for him. On Monday at recess the cousins punched the boy and the rest of the boys in the class helped the boy. Everyone came together to stand up against the cousins by telling the teachers and principal about what was going on and the cousins got expelled. A male middle school student shared that "there's rumors on Facebook, oh, you are a lesbian or slut stuff like that." These student comments reveal that sexuality and promiscuity can play a major role in cyberbullying activity at times.

Appearance and money were also mentioned by students as to why some individuals cyberbully others. Being different during the middle and high school years can provide fodder for being cyberbullied. A female middle school participant said that in her old school a girl picked on an overweight girl by posting comments on Facebook saying, "she's going to blow up if she keeps eating." She kept posting and the overweight girl eventually just ignored the postings. At a time in life where things like appearance are important to status and having friends, comments like these can be detrimental to a teenager's psyche.

Having material possessions and money were also cited as something cyberbullies tended to pick on. A female middle school student said that she got in a fight with a girl because she was talking about her family. This girl called her a "low-lifer" and made fun of her because her family did not have any money. The two girls went back and forth on Facebook posting on each other's walls saying mean things. The focus group participant said that she engaged in cyberbullying behavior saying, "when I get mad I can't stop." This brings up an interesting aspect of cyberbullying. At what point does a victim also become a cyberbully? In an open-ended questionnaire response a high school student said: "I never cyberbullied someone who didn't do anything to deserve it. If they do something to me, then I'm coming back 10 times harder." This reveals a reciprocal nature to the cyberbullying phenomenon where victims come back to cyberbully the original cyberbully, which can be very different from physical bullying. Also some well-intentioned friends that come to the aid of a friend in need also can contribute to a cyberbullying situation. In an open-ended questionnaire response a high school student said: "I have never really cyberbullied anybody. I just either defend others being cyberbullied or address a problem that involved me." However, in coming to the defense of a friend or in defending yourself in a manner that mimics the cyberbully's, it in essence becomes a cyberbullying act as well.

Students were also asked who was most likely to start problems online. Middle school focus group participants thought that it had something to do with age:

Female Focus Group Participant: It's more 8th grade.

Focus Group Moderator: Why do you think it's more with 8th graders than 7th graders?

Male Focus Group Participant: They are like kids that are more mature and think oh, I have high school friends. Just because they have friends that are older and they think they are more mature and they can do stuff.

High school students agreed that it was the younger students that caused a lot of the cyberbullying problems:

> **Female Focus Group Participant:** It's like sometimes Freshmen they sit there and talk about a person. Like most of the times with the girls it will be like jealousy.
>
> **Male Focus Group Participant:** If you are at school it is tough, because most of the rumors start off with Freshmans. I analyzed this, they all start with the Freshmen then they go spreading that thing. When you come to the Upper classman I guess they build some maturity or they realize how much [name of school] is and that's how the rumors are that's how I would react. I would go straight to the person hey, you were talking of that stuff what is that?

Besides being in the eighth or ninth grade students thought that females were more likely to be involved in cyberbullying activity:

> **Male Focus Group Participant:** Mostly like 8th grade not as much in 7th grade...it's like between the girls and then if it's guys it's like you are the biggest whopper, something like that.

This student indicated that females were more likely to be in a bigger online dispute than males who would just call each other names and be done with it. When asked what kind of person or groups tended to do the cyberbullying, middle school students said:

> **Female Focus Group Participant:** It's like a whole group, like a kid will chip in from a group, I don't know.
>
> **Male Focus Group Participant:** It's not a group...so there's a couple popular and couple jocks or something. Usually people that get good grades and stuff don't do that it's mostly people who like attention on them, stuff like that.

Students indicated that there are different cliques in school and sometimes a person from a clique will engage in cyberbullying, but it does not necessarily mean that the whole group is in a battle with another group. Students were aware of the students in their school were most likely to be cyberbullies. They indicated that individuals who did well in school were less likely to cyberbully others, while those that liked attention were more likely to enable drama and engage in cyberbullying behavior.

Chapter Summary

Students revealed a conceptualization issue regarding cyberbullying that could shed light on the discrepancies in the literature regarding perpetration and victimization rates. If students are unaware of what behaviors constitute cyberbullying and where the boundaries are between jokes and bullying, one can imagine their survey responses in any study—especially when terms like cyberbullying are not defined—to not accurately represent the situation. Students also reported a number of ways cyberbullying occurred (e.g., though social network status messages, social network groups, pictures, videos, etc.) and factors (e.g., sexuality, promiscuity, jealousy, physical appearance, etc.) that contributed to cyberbullying engagement. Most telling, students communicated a sense of overlap between their online and school environments.

CHAPTER 7

Consequences Related to Cyberbullying

> "I have been a victim of cyberbullying before and I really don't know how it started. Some girls just started saying many things about me for many years and it got to the point where one of my reletives [sic] were shot and killed. When this happened the girls kept going on with the names on Facebook so after I moved I deleted my account and made a new one." – Female middle school student

Our study also sought to provide answers regarding how cyberbullying impacted those involved. In the following subsections we will share student narratives describing how cyberbullying has affected victims, their friends, and their siblings.

DIFFERENT PEOPLE, DIFFERENT WAYS

Students reported that they thought cyberbullying impacted different people in different ways. In an entry from an open-ended questionnaire item a high school student wrote about how cyberbullying made her not want to go to school:

> It wasn't necessarily the cyberbullying that made me not want to go, it was just the presence of the other people. I'm the kind who is focused, so I go to school to learn, and like socialize of course, it was just the drama that made me not want to go to school. Like people talking, it gets to a point were you do have to listen to it, you do get offended, and I didn't want to go to school because I couldn't learn/socialize/do what I actually wanted to do. *(note: the participant indicated emphasis with underlining)*

This student wanted to go to school because he/she liked the school environment because it offered him/her the opportunity to both learn and socialize. However, this excitement can be deterred by people who commit cyberbullying acts as the things that they write and say can become something that is seen as inescapable. In response to an open-ended questionnaire item a middle school student reported the following observation:

> Yes, cyberbullying has created a problem since "my friends" [have] been backstabbing me [and] they continued to do it at school. And for that reason I couldn't concentrate because I was thinking of ways of how I could get back at them which was not smart.

These things can make it difficult to concentrate during classes and become a distraction during the school day. A high school student wrote in this regard:

> Yes, it obstructed my learning…like when I went to school and everybody was talking about me, because this boy liked me, or whatever, so I couldn't learn, my friends were turning against from me, so it made me feel like left out on my own.

Besides becoming a distraction to learning, cyberbullying can also make students feel alone, as cyberbullies and cyberbully victims may even be friends with one another. With other friends in common, friends often choose sides in fights—thereby leaving someone to feel left out.

Students indicated that they themselves had not skipped school due to cyberbullying activity, but could see how they might be affected that way and have heard of cases where cyberbullying caused students to skip school. During a focus group session with high school students a male group participant remarked that he did not see a lot of people skipping school due to cyberbullying, but rather wanted to come to school to address the situation:

> I don't think that happens here personally…everybody claims that something like that happens they automatically have to find out. It's more like people are eager to come to school so they can address the situation. I can't wait to get to school so I can see if so and so said this and I don't know anybody who

> honestly skipped school because they are scared of what people are going to think. There are probably people who get here and after it gets around they hear how bad it is they start to become emotionally upset and break down and cry or something like that.

Instead of making students not want to go to school, cyberbullying can have the opposite effect in that it makes students want to go to school to get a more comprehensive understanding of the situation. However, once they try to address the situation, it can end up making them emotionally upset.

Other students in their written responses agreed with the male focus group participant's statement. A middle school student wrote: "if I do get in a fight with someone I want to talk it out." A high school student also agreed by writing: "I address issues and whatever the issue is, it is what it is." Another high school student wrote that: "I wanted to go to school because of gossip to keep the argument going to defend myself." Even though some students like to address issues and defend themselves, it can affect other students differently. Middle school focus group participants spoke about how going to school after being cyberbullied can make you feel afraid:

> **Female Focus Group Participant:** Like seeing them and being afraid what's going to happen next.
>
> **Male Focus Group Participant:** I think it's scary for them because they know people have seen that stuff.

In an open-ended questionnaire a middle school student wrote:

> Yeah, a group of 8th graders were like saying all this mean stuff to me. I see them everyday so I didn't want to go to school. I felt like they were gonna come up to me and say those mean things.

When students have been a cyberbullying victim it can make some of them afraid to go to school as they do not know how the person that cyberbullied them is going to act and treat them in person. Also, as the male focus group participant indicated, it is scary and intimidating to go to school knowing that many of the other students you see on a daily basis have seen the text messages or Facebook posts causing them concern.

These situations can manifest themselves in different ways. As indicated above, cyberbullying can create a feeling of being alone or can become a major distraction that can make it difficult to concentrate in school. Besides loneliness and distractions, cyberbullying can also create situations that manifest in threats to physical safety. In an open-ended questionnaire entry a high school student remarked that he/she had not gotten in a physical fight due to cyberbullying, but "many friends have had arguments or even physical fights." A female middle school focus group participant told a story she heard from her sister: "My sister said that in high school there was this one girl who posted something with her pictures in it and they got into a fight—a cat fight."

This student illustrates that a situation that starts in cyberspace—like posting pictures on Facebook—can end up in a physical alteration in the school environment. Another middle school female focus group participant commented on this as well: "In different schools I've been in some girls posted stuff on another girl's wall and they actually were big fights so they have strict codes." Things like pictures and comments posted on another person's Facebook wall can provoke physical altercations in the school environment—so much so that many schools have had to create policy and implement codes of conduct regarding cyberbullying activity.

While cyberbullying can lead to distractions in the classroom and physical fights in the hallways, it can also have life-altering consequences for some students. For some students engaging in cyberbullying activity the experience can lead to having to transfer schools. A female middle school focus group participant shared a story about her brother:

> He was on MySpace and then there was this person that didn't like my brother that much. And then they were fighting on the Internet. I don't know for what and then they ended up in a fight at school. But my brother didn't want to deal with that because he wanted to keep studying and stuff. And so he eventually had to transfer schools because he [the other boy] wouldn't stop stalking him. So he canceled his account and made a different one.

Even though this student portrays her brother as a cyberbullying victim, he had to remove himself from his school environment, cancel his MySpace account, and reestablish a new one in order to stop the act of cyberbullying from reoccurring. In response to an open-ended questionnaire item a middle school student wrote the following in this regard:

> People were saying stuff behind my back. Like I was a bad friend and other inappropriate names… through MySpace. It made me feel angry and depressed because if I was being a bad friend then why did they even bother to talk to me? I stopped talking to them and changed schools.

Social network environments, such as Facebook and MySpace, provide a convenient forum for individuals to easily post comments that can be hurtful to others without having to say these things directly to their face. This type of cowardice can leave victims feeling angry, depressed, and as if they could not function in that school environment any longer. A group of middle school focus group participants told a story about how face-to-face bullying and cyberbullying can make victims feel like their very life is being threatened. There were twin girls who attended their school that bullied and threatened everyone. It got serious when the twin girls starting bullying a particular girl at their school. After gym they took her shoe and skirt. Outside of school they posted social network status messages, calling her a "B" [participants indicated an expletive]. Then the twins said their brother, who is in a gang, was going to come after her. The twins ended up getting kicked out and the girl left, as she was no longer comfortable in that particular school environment. The participants wished she would not have left because they liked and missed her.

However, disturbing situations can progress even further than can be reminded by leaving a schooling environment and transferring to another. In response to an open-ended questionnaire item a middle school student shared an experience he/she had where cyberbullying acts built up over years:

> I have been a victim of cyberbullying before and I really don't know how it started. Some girls just started saying many things about me for <u>many years</u> and it got to the point where

> one of my reletives [sic] were shot and killed. When this happened the girls kept going on with the names on Facebook so after I moved I deleted my account and made a new one. *(note: the participant indicated emphasis with underlining)*

This student's powerful story is quite clear, moving, and tragic. Many times students do not know how cyberbullying starts, but it builds up and progresses over time. In the case of this student, something that started off as a simple case of girls saying things about him/her spun out of control to the point where a relative of his/hers was murdered. Cyberbullying can alter the lives of some of those who participate in it. It can cause students to transfer schools and rebuild their friend networks. During a cyberbullying act, threats can be made to make victims fear for their physical safety, an action which can scar them socially and emotionally. At the scariest of times threats to one's physical safety made online and in person can become a reality making it possible for a life-threatening action to become a loss of life.

STUDENT FEARS REGARDING CYBERBULLYING

In their open-ended questionnaire entries some students wrote that cyberbullying made them feel scared, sad, and sometimes depressed. A middle school student wrote the following along these lines:

> Actually I was even scared to go on my email because I did not want to see what people had been saying about me. It made me feel depressed because I started to think that maybe they were right and I was a bad friend! Which I was NOT!

Cyberbullying can make people afraid to interact with others the ways they typically are used to. As in the case of this student, it may make them afraid to check email or their social network sites, fearing what they might see a message from the perpetrators. Another student indicated that it was difficult dealing with "the feeling when people are mad/hate you." A different middle school student wrote that it made them "depressed, but never far enough to commit suicide." High school students were less likely to indicate that cyberbullying had made them depressed. Their entries reflected that they dealt with problems as they arose, and used the experience of victimization as a learning experience. For example, one student wrote: "I got over it and I still remember how it all happened, but I just tried to avoid it."

Some students were more aware of cyberbullying and participation in the behavior than others. In an open-ended questionnaire entry a high school student wrote: "I haven't used a social network to bully anyone because I wouldn't want anyone to bully me." This student seemed to have a good understanding of treating people the way you want to be treated, and that he/she would not cyberbully others because he/she did not want to be put in that position. Unfortunately, other students were not as sure. In an open-ended questionnaire entry that asked if they had cyberbullied anyone in the past, a high school student wrote: "No, and if so it wasn't intentional." At times students may be under the impression that they are not cyberbullying others when they may in fact be doing so. This means that the reverse may also be true—that students could be unknowingly victimized. A middle school student wrote: "if someone posted something on my wall, I probably took it the wrong way. It's mostly more joking around than anything really bad." This brings up an important aspect in that whether or not someone feels bullied is partly based on perception of those involved. A high school student wrote that "it's stupid how people get offended by the smallest things." However, it could also reflect a situation where the victims blame themselves for taking things too personally, even though the things that were said were not appropriate. This leads to an interesting question this study raises in asking where is the line? What is to be taken as joking around and what is to be taken as cyberbullying?

CHAPTER SUMMARY

Students reported a mix of feelings regarding the impact of cyberbullying that included feeling scared, sad, and even depressed. They shared their own stories, their friends' stories, and their sibling's stories regarding how cyberbullying can inhibit concentration while at school and even lead to physical altercations. They also revealed stories that conveyed clear consequences to cyberbullying engagement (e.g., needing to transfer school), as well as experiences that were far more dangerous (e.g., relatives being murdered) than expected.

CHAPTER 8

Coping With Cyberbullying

> "You know say I go to the teacher or something. Then the teacher, they monitor the situation and they have to follow the procedures. People are going to find out how I ended up snitching out. That leads to more bullying on me so everyone is calling me scary and fake and that will get me more mad."-- Male high school student

During focus group sessions students also offered their strategies for dealing with cyberbullying. Students provided good perspective on this issue, noting that their response strategy would depend on the situation; they noted both active and passive tactics for dealing with cyberbullying victimization.

IT DEPENDS...

Some students reported that it depended on the situation as to how they would react if they or someone they knew was involved in a cyberbullying situation. Students indicated that it depended on who was involved as to how they would react:

> **Female Focus Group Participant 1:** It also depends on what kind of friends you have.
>
> **Female Focus Group Participant 2:** Because you see that happening like normally so you might just say she's always in trouble and that maybe is just your friend or you might see something that's not common for her. If she's a friend that normally doesn't get into fights or anything you might go in to help her. Sometimes you choose friends that you are not supposed to choose and are not good for you and if you see that happening almost twice a day. You might stop being friends with her.

As these students indicated, there are some students that are more likely to engage in cyberbullying behavior than others. When students are friends with students who regularly engage in behavior that causes trouble, they would be less likely to help him/her. Further, if they see a consistent pattern developing regarding a friend's behavior they may terminate the friendship, as it was not good for them to be friends with a troublemaker. However, if the friend engaged in the cyberbullying situation was not typically in trouble or causing trouble, they would be more likely to step in to help that friend.

Students also indicated that how they would react to cyberbullying—either to their friends or to themselves—would depend on the particular situation. A male high school student reported that if a friend was involved in a cyberbullying incident he would take his friend's feelings and desire regarding the situation into account before acting: "It depends on the situation, how they might feel about it and how they might respond. If I'm close to them I'd set it off, if not, I'd let it go." This student also reveals that the closeness of the relationship also plays a part in how a friend might react to the situation. A close friend would be willing to stick up for a friend and confront the perpetrator, while with an acquaintance you may not feel like that reaction would be appropriate. Another male high school student shared that he thought it also depended on how far the situation escalated:

> I think it depends on how far it escalates. If it escalates to that point…I'm not going to automatically say "let's box." I was raised in that type of environment but …I realize not to do that. But if it does get to that point you have no choice. It gets to the point where everybody is so fed up to just approach you, you have no choice but to defend yourself.

Even though this student said that he was raised in an environment that condoned physical altercations as a solution to problems, he thought it was best to not automatically go to that point. Instead, he advised that it was important to think of other options. At times, however, he argued that there was a point where there were no other choices but to have to defend yourself.

Some students gave concrete examples about what they would do if they saw a particular cyberbullying act occurring to a friend or themselves. In a middle school focus group students generally agreed that if someone was just calling them names then they would not do anything. However, if it was more serious (e.g., threats like breaking windows/coming to house to hurt you or a lot of people involved) then they would tell an adult or parent. This was just a snippet of what the young people that were spoken to cited as ways to deal with cyberbullying activity. In the subsequent sections, further evidence of passive (e.g., do nothing, ignore it, etc.) and active (e.g., tell someone, defend yourself, etc.) strategies will be documented.

PASSIVE STRATEGIES

Students reported using a variety of passive strategies to deal with cyberbullying activity. For many, dealing with rumors and gossip requires using a strategy that focuses on whom one trusts. A female high school student spoke to this aspect during a focus group session:

> …you know you can't tell everybody your personal business. When I come to school every day I see a lot of people doing that—whatever they did with their friend, their boyfriend and they come to the friend…and basically it's going to go round school you know.

This student points out an interesting aspect of dealing with cyberbullying activity. Often, engagement can be passively prevented by understanding whom to trust. By revealing personal things about themselves to individuals who may not be able to keep information to themselves, students leave themselves vulnerable to cyberbullying attacks associated with rumors and gossip. Students also indicated that the credibility of the person doing the cyberbullying through spreading the gossip and rumors was important:

> **Female Focus Group Participant:** I hear gossip from certain people. Like somebody was talking about how their ex-boyfriend was crying over them or something and they're not really that reliable of a person. So I'm like, I don't really believe you, why are you talking about him that kind of thing.

If a student that was likely to want to make up something about the cyberbullying victim, as in the case of an ex-boyfriend/girlfriend relationship, students were less likely to view the information as credible. Therefore, the victim was likely to be less affected with the understanding that those reading and hearing the information would not believe what was being said.

Some students indicated that it was necessary to think before acting when it came to engaging in a cyberbullying situation. A male high school student reported that individuals often act out of anger before thinking: "I think they act out of anger before they actually stop and think why it's being said and if they actually know if it's true or not." Both victims and other individuals reading the messages tend to act out of anger before thinking about the situation. This can create quick reactions that can further escalate the incident. However, students also revealed that in many cases they did nothing and did their best to not let gossip, rumors, and cyberbullying bother them. When it came to friends who were being cyberbullied, students revealed that they tried to stay out of it when possible. A male middle school focus group participant said: "Stay out of it? Yeah otherwise you get roped into it."

While some students said that they would defend their friends, others knew that defending their friend would get them further involved in the undesirable cyberbullying activity. Ignoring the situation was a popular response when it came to tactics to deal with cyberbullying. A female high school student thought that if people have problems with her, they should talk to her about it and if they could not do that she would ignore them:

> I like to say that if you have problems with somebody just go to that person and talk to them. Sometimes they talk about me like why she always dressed like that. I'm here why don't you just come to me and ask me a question like why are you wearing this or why do you do what you do. That's why there are problems...they just think about themselves. If I had this problem I would want them to come to me...They think it's cool to talk about other people and make fun of other people...I'll be looking at them and I'm like OK, I am going to ignore you.

When students are in some way different (e.g., obese, from a different culture) from a majority of the student population it puts them at risk of being talked about at school and cyberbullied beyond school walls. With students wanting to be like everyone else and wanting to gain friendships, as well as achieve recognition in the school, they may turn to making fun of other people. As a passive technique, those with a high level of self-esteem and sense of pride find it easier to ignore these individuals.

A few students mentioned passive tactics that included being proud of yourself and focused on self-esteem. A female high school student spoke about being proud of yourself in this context in this focus group excerpt:

> I look at people sometimes. I don't hang out with a lot of people, a lot of people don't know me. I look at people to know who they are because I am who I am and I'm proud of myself being who I am. But some people don't realize who they are and they keep making fun out of people who are being themselves.

This student conveyed a sense of pride in who she was that helped to shield her from engaging in cyberbullying activity. This pride also seemed to give her an understanding that people without this pride may lash out at others, as they might be more likely to try to fit in with their peers. In response to an open-ended questionnaire item a high school student shared that he/she had not been cyberbullied, but if he/she were they "wouldn't take what they said to heart anyways." In another entry a high school student wrote: "I hear rumors about me every so often; I don't let it bother me because I have a high self esteem." Like the pride the female high school focus group participant spoke about, self-esteem can also shield individuals from cyberbullying as it allows them to brush off things because they are satisfied with themselves.

Active Strategies

Students also revealed active strategies for dealing with cyberbullying victimization to themselves or their friends. Some students indicated that they would actively work to "find out who started the rumor." Others said that they would read the postings or messages, but would delete them. A male high school focus group participant said that many things would not spiral out of proportion if people would just actively address issues when they came up:

> I'm the type to address the issue. Like the last class period, like half the classroom was laughing at one of my friends when they were talking about her. I was like they are talking about your shoes do you want us to set it off or not and she was like no and the teacher was like OK you need to calm down during the class so it just ended right there. So, I think people should just start addressing things instead of just going around talking about it. Just address the issue, what you so scared about.

As this student points out, if situations are actively mitigated they are less likely to wind up online in a cyberbullying situation and escalate further. A few students reported that they would "teach them [cyberbullying perpetrators] a lesson." During focus groups sessions "teaching them a lesson" was revealed to take the form of confronting the perpetrator or defending themselves or their friend who was victimized in other ways. If a friend was being cyberbullied a female high school student said she would first see if the friend was okay and then confront the perpetrator:

> If someone was talking about my friends I probably would talk to my friend and say are you OK. Whoever the person was I would confront them. I'm not like, I want to fight you I would be like why is it necessary for you to talk about them, what have they done to you. I would be like you shouldn't be talking about anybody. I would tell them that it's real childish talking about them behind their back and telling other people [things].

While this student said she would not fight the perpetrator physically, she indicated that she would confront them verbally. However, verbal altercations can escalate as well. A female high school student said that "when you confront a person about a rumor they automatically assume the worst and get defensive." A male high school student shared the following:

> People have tried messing with me, but I'm not the kind of person who will let someone run over me. I'm going to defend myself. When it becomes physical I'm going to defend myself. I'm not going to stay quiet. I'm not that person.

When people get defensive tempers, can flare and some people may react to a cyberbullying situation in a physical manner.

Some students indicated that when friends got into a cyberbullying incident that they tried not to get involved. A female middle school student reported: "I would like to help them, but I would not like to get involved with that because they might start taking it against you. And you don't want to get involved." While students indicated that they would like to help friends, they also did not want to draw attention to themselves becoming the brunt of the perpetrator's cyberbullying behavior. By getting involved friends of cyberbullying victims can create problems for themselves, or even make the original problem worse. Sometimes students felt like they were caught in the middle:

> **Female Middle School Student:** You are in the middle because it's like you are my friend you should be backing me up, you know what I mean. And the other way, I don't want to get into trouble so I won't help. Sometimes you do the thing that's right and something goes wrong.

Friends of cyberbullying victims often feel like they are in a no-win situation as they feel pressure to come to the defense of their friend, but at the same time do not want to get in trouble for trying to help. When cyberbullied, it may become difficult to not defend yourself or your friend:

> **Female Middle School Student:** ...sometimes they say something and you don't do anything about it and just let it go and other times they say something and keep going until you finally, like, say something back.

As this student indicated, there are times when students try to do nothing and avoid provoking the cyberbully. However, when the cyberbully does not let up this often forces the victim to engage in the retaliatory cyberbullying activity, further perpetuating the situation.

Students were not in agreement as to if they would tell anyone about the cyberbullying behaviors they know about. They also disagreed on if they had to tell someone if cyberbullying was happening to them or a friend, and who that someone would be. A female middle school student said that she knew she probably should tell her parents if she was victimized by a cyberbullying perpetrator, but was afraid to do so: "I would think I should tell my parents all this stuff, but they would get angry with me or tell the school or something." While this student knew that she should probably tell her parents when she was victimized by a cyberbully, she was unsure if she actually would as she was concerned that they would get angry with her—perhaps revoking her social network or cell phone privileges—or take it to the school level where she may have to confront the cyberbully. This could create even more problems, as another student noted:

> **Male High School Focus Group Participant**: You know say I go to the teacher or something. Then the teacher, they monitor the situation and they have to follow the procedures. People are going to find out how I ended up snitching out. That leads to more bullying on me so everyone is calling me scary and fake and that will get me more mad.

If information gets to the school level it can create a situation where it gets out that the victim told –or "snitched out"—on the perpetrator. This has potential to spur further problems with the cyberbully and with the school population as it goes against group norms to deal with these situations on your own as they arise and to not get school personnel involved.

There were other issues regarding telling school personnel as well. A male high school student said: "I don't trust my teachers." This could be due to various reasons. Some students told stories about school personnel trying to create fake teenage profiles to friend students in the school's network to keep an eye on what they post. Other students talked about how they did not feel like teachers had power to help them with cyberbullying acts on an individual level. A female high school student reported: "...students don't tell teachers a lot also because they follow protocol using the disciplinarian of the school." A male high school student agreed with this observation saying: "I don't know if people actually go tell the teacher because a lot of teachers they follow protocol or procedures and I know that every situation should be handled that way." As teachers needed to follow a certain protocol they were not allowed to help students on an individual basis based on the situations and students' varying needs. Instead, they had to report the activity to the disciplinarian of the school who followed further protocol that included further acts like talking it out and punishment (e.g., detention, suspension, expulsion, etc.).

Some students felt like it was not a teacher's job to deal with things that happened on Facebook. A female middle school student indicated: "I don't think teachers…like dealing with that stuff because it's more of a parent thing. They are the ones who give permission beyond that so I think teachers don't want to deal with it." A female high school student also spoke about this issue, indicating that she would tell her parents over teachers:

> I would go to my mom or dad because my mom, she tells me, she said you can talk to me about anything. And how we were talking about the teachers—I really wouldn't go to teacher that is like extremely bad or dangerous or something like that because it's just too much for the teachers. If the situation were like my mom if she asked me is it OK do I need to come to your school, do I need to go to the office then I would tell her if she could come.

With limited power as to what happens outside of school grounds, students thought that because parents controlled what happens to their children after school they were responsible to monitor after school Facebook use and were more capable of diffusing dangerous situations.

High school students were more likely than middle school students to report that they would tell a parent. A male high school student said that he would tell his mom:

> If it gets to the point I would tell my mom because I talk to my mom a lot as a friend and I tell her this is going on, such and such. Because I know she is not going to bash me out or cases like you don't need to be doing this or she give me the advice that she would give some of her friends. Or if she was in my shoes.

Parents—especially moms—were cited as being the ones to go to if a student felt like he/she was truly in trouble. They felt that their moms were likely to give them advice instead of punishing them. Another male high school student talked about how his mom gives him advice:

> I mean I talk to my Mom. When I have problems like that I just call her and tell her and she'd be like you got to know what to do, you got to manage people how they treat you…every time I talk to my mom I get more ideas about how to treat people.

Parents hold many keys to teaching their children about how to treat people and act in adverse situations. However, some students were at odds over whether adults would understand their lives:

> **Male Focus Group Participant 1:** Sometimes even by going to people it don't really help because some like—'specially adults—most of the adults don't know how teenagers are these days. So it's hard for teachers to give advice or counselors to give advice to teenagers because the way they handled situations when they were younger is different from now. It's hard to understand the teenagers nowadays because they know everything with new technology… everything is different.

> **Male Focus Group Participant 2:** I really don't think things have changed. I think, I'm not going to lie my parents were teens once, too. They must have wanted to go out and have fun and be crazy.

Every generation thinks that their parents have no idea what they are going through, but the second student points out that while the medium might change parents and teachers were once the same age and have gone through different versions of the same problems they face. One student said that it depended on where she was as to who she would go to:

> **Female High School Focus Group Participant:** It depends where I am. For example if I'm at school I'll go with the teacher I trust the most, but when I'm at home I'll go with my

> parents or my family. If I'm somewhere else like I'm hanging out with my friends I'll go to my friends who I trust the most.

This student reflects that the person she would tell would be dependent on the environment she was physically in when the cyberbullying act occurred. Given that middle school students were less likely to tell their parents, they reported going to others first:

> **Focus Group Moderator:** Who would you guys tell if you tell somebody?
>
> **Male Focus Group Participant 1:** Probably my sister, because she's older or probably one of my friends.
>
> **Male Focus Group Participant 2:** I'd tell my sister and a last resort my parents.

If students needed to get advice on what to do about a cyberbullying situation they were likely to go to an older sibling, a trusted friend, and as a last resort their parents. Middle school students also reported a high level of family monitoring. Several female participants indicated that they were friends with parents or close family members (e.g., siblings, cousins, uncles) that monitored their Facebook accounts. For the most part these participants said that they had "nothing to hide" and it did not bother them. A female middle school focus group participant said that her brother monitored her Facebook:

> …my brother, he tells me he won't let me get a Facebook or MySpace account. I don't even have MySpace, I have Facebook. But he told me all the things. He has me as a friend so he checks my Facebook wall…

She went on to share a story about how her brother hacked into her Facebook account:

> It's quite annoying because he never asked me and I never gave him my password. He literally went to my account 'cause I had left it somewhere and I have a key to get that password. He got it and got on my Facebook and he started checking my

> friends. I noticed that some of my friends were deleted and then I understood why. Then he told me what was I looking for outside I didn't need to be friends with them because he deleted seven of them. Yeah I got mad at him. I didn't talk to him for some time.

Family members can easily hack into other family members accounts as they often can guess passwords or know information that may be asked in security questions to unlock a password. In the case of this student, her brother utilized his knowledge to gain access to her Facebook friend list to prune the people he did not see fit to be his sister's friends.

Schools also offered options that students thought had the potential to decrease cyberbullying activity. After the focus group session at the high school, a male senior shared that before the school year had started the school offered a senior retreat that featured activities aimed at students getting to know one another. He said that he had seen a program on MTV that had students from different friend groups spend time with one another and get to know each other. At the end of the show students reflected on what they had learned about each other and the things that they had in common. This student thought that when you really get to know fellow students that you come to realize that you have things in common which makes you less likely to make fun of or bully them. While he thought it was a nice event to put on for seniors, that it might be more effective for all students—especially freshmen—to take part in as an effective deterrent to cyberbullying.

CHAPTER SUMMARY

Students reported a number of coping strategies employed when they witnessed or were victimized by cyberbullying behavior. Students indicated that their reaction highly depended on the situation and who was involved. For example, if a close friend who was not known for engaging in cyberbullying activity was victimized, students indicated that they would be more likely to intervene to defend and support them. Finally, students revealed various approaches—both passively and actively—that they coped when they were victimized by cyberbullying behavior. Students stated they might do nothing and ignore the cyberbullying behavior if it was not serious. However, if it was serious enough they might tell someone like a trusted friend, sibling, relative, or parent.

CHAPTER 9

School Staff Views on Social Technology and Cyberbullying

> "I don't believe Facebook is a bad thing. Facebook is a tool just like a wrench, a pen or pencil—those are all tools. And that's how I look at Facebook."—School staff member

After students participated in focus groups, school staff were also asked about their perceptions related to social technology and cyberbullying in their schools. The following themes emerged: *Facebook problems and cyberbullying*; *school policy, rules, and protocol*; *need for a prevention program*; and *other related thoughts*. Under these themes various topics surfaced that were both similar and dissimilar from student opinion. After these themes are discussed, student and staff perceptions of social technology and cyberbullying issues will be compared and contrasted.

FACEBOOK PROBLEMS AND CYBERBULLYING ISSUES

School staff members were asked which social technologies students typically used. From their perspective, texting and Facebook were the most popular among their students. However, they generally noted that students also used Twitter, a microblogging website, and email. Staff members hypothesized that nearly 90% of their respective students were on Facebook, and soon virtually all would be. Facebook incorporates individuals declaring connections to other people and deeming them as "friends." During focus group sessions a school staff member reflected on what a "friend" of this type was:

> That's the funny thing about our terminology of friends with them calling them friends on Facebook. I'm like you're really nice, but you don't have 1,500 friends—maybe 25, maybe 30 of those are real friends and probably not even that many.

> They will be friends because they go to the same school. They don't even associate with the person here at school whatsoever. Facebook has suggestions because they have mutual friends or they go to [this school] they accept them as a friend. I sometimes try to explain the difference what a friend actually is. I tell them I have genuine friends on my friend list. I even got a picture of his daughter at her birthday party, this is a friend, I know his last name. Or I know his real name.

During student focus groups some participants reported having up to 4,000 friends. In the interview excerpt above this staff member spoke to this by talking about the term. Students are friends with people on Facebook that they might not be genuinely friends with in person. Instead, they add fellow schoolmates and other individuals their already associated "friends" may have connected to via the mutual friends feature on Facebook. This school staff member went on to share how students may not differentiate between genuine friends and Facebook "friends":

> Sometimes I have to deal with students telling me stories and I'm like please don't use nicknames, please don't. Ashley by the way which is the most common name in the world, Ashley, I'm like which Ashley could you be a bit more specific. What grade is she in, can you tell me more what she looks like, it's Ashley. They start out with my friend Ashley I'm like if that's a friend why don't you know her last name. Then they admit we just hang around; we are not really friends. What really shocked me that they have each other's phone numbers and not be good friends. That's stuff I have to figure out with you, I understand Facebook but I don't quite understand how there is a exchange of phone numbers, but they never call each other. That's something I'm still working on. It happens more than you would think.

When students "friend" other teenagers they do not know very well it can create issues for school staff when problems among students arise on Facebook. As this staff member indicates, there is confusion over how one can be "friends" on Facebook and even have one another's phone number, but not really know each other. This was a large difference between students and school staff. In a school staff focus group session a participant talked about how her friends were known:

> I have been on for a while so I have a couple hundred, but these are people that I actually know. Someone said to me something and I'm like I have no idea who this is so I'm going to unfriend them. Even a couple I know, they are from high school and I'll see mutual friends, but I'm like they don't remember you so therefore, forget it.

Instead of friending people they may have met once or had known a long time ago adults tend to stick to friending people they know well. One school staff focus group participant indicated that she was "old school" and did not "have time for that stuff [Facebook]. However, when school staff were on Facebook they were very cognizant of who they were friends with and reported setting up boundaries on who they would add:

> My policy for myself personally is that I will not friend any student that is a current student at [this school]. I have students that have graduated and that are in college. I don't seek any of them out at all, but if they request me and they are already a non-student then I will friend them. Not if they are currently a student here.

As they added people and students they knew they also commented that they censored themselves for appropriateness. A female school staff member shared:

> I'm really careful about what I put out there. I mean I never put anything about 'oh, work sucks' you know what I mean. Anything I put out there is usually something about my kids or nothing political, nothing religious, none of that stuff.

As authority figures, school staff made sure to never mention work on Facebook or to not be controversial when it came to politics and religion. Besides creating boundaries for themselves on adding people they knew well and prior students, school staff also made sure to set their privacy settings high so people they didn't know and current students could not access their personal information. They indicated that setting high privacy settings was a major difference between them and students: "…the privacy settings are not real high at all probably. They don't know, they don't care, they just put it all up there."

When students do not set their privacy settings high (e.g., to only allow "friends" to view their information) the general public can access their information, which provides further opportunity for cyberbullying victimization by perpetrators they know minimally or not at all. This aspect of Facebook is an important one which school-based authorities and parents can have influence over with teenagers if they decide to do so.

Even though Facebook can cause serious problems for school staff, they did not see it necessarily as a bane to their school environment. A school staff member reflected on how Facebook is neither a good nor bad thing inherently. Instead, it is like any tool and the way it is used defines its utility or, alternatively, its dangers. One school staff member noted the following in this regard:

> I don't believe Facebook is a bad thing. Facebook is a tool just like a wrench, a pen or pencil—those are all tools. And that's how I look at Facebook. I usually keep in touch with friends all over the country, the world–just to keep in touch. They do it sometimes also, unfortunately sometimes they use it as a form or tool to speak their mind. Which people have in their mind, you know, this is my right to do whatever I want to. Well you can't say whatever you want to unless you can take the consequences of whatever you are going to say. I don't think, I don't believe they always keep that in mind.

Facebook has the potential to create, expand, and maintain friendships locally, nationally, and even around the world. Unfortunately, being behind a computer screen can help mask potential consequences—especially for youth. A school staff member offered further explanation in this regard:

> I think there are problems associated with Facebook. I can't say Facebook is a problem. I joke with my colleagues all the time how much I hate Facebook. If it didn't exist how much easier my life would be. I will say that it may just magnify

> issues that currently exist. Bullying isn't a new thing at all. I think because of Facebook maybe an individual who would not believe they might do it they can hide behind a computer screen so to speak.

While Facebook causes many problems in the middle and high schools, it is not problematic in itself. Without Facebook, bullying, gossip, and rumors would still exist. However, what is problematic is how Facebook can magnify a situation and how it gives individuals who would normally not involve themselves in verbal or physical altercations the power to do so through the perceived anonymity of hiding behind a computer screen.

School staff members talked at length about how things that happen in school are magnified on Facebook, and *vice versa*. Often the face-to-face and Facebook overlap results in cyberbullying activity among their middle and high school students. Since students share the same school environment and "friend" each other on Facebook, altercations can emerge at school which arise from their interaction through this social medium. A school staff member indicated that cyberbullying that takes place outside of school can affect students during school: "Sometimes arguing in class. I know there have been a couple of physical altercations because of it but I don't see that a lot." Cyberbullying engagement can cause arguing and, if particularly intense, physical altercations during school. These altercations affect not only the students involved, but the broader learning environment as well.

School staff members reported that they have noticed that when altercations happen in school, based on cyberbullying activity, that they are unaware of what cyberbullying is or how to define it. A school staff member explained:

> I think that it happens a lot more than we hear about. I mean I'm sure it's going on way more than what is coming to us. It might not all be as major as what we are hearing. But I just feel like look at what she was wearing today, that type of thing, where it's not always that slanderous but I think that it happens a lot and I think the students don't even really identify that as bullying sometimes.

School staff hear about only a handful of cyberbullying cases, as many such experiences go unreported. Many of the stories school staff and students hear focus on the dire consequences sometimes associated with cyberbullying (e.g., suicide). However, the minor cases (e.g., rumors and gossip) happen much more frequently and are something that students are unlikely to even define as cyberbullying. A female school staff member spoke to this point: "Because with bullying…a lot of times [they] got beat up [and] got pushed. Sometimes they don't even think words are bullying. I have a feeling that they don't feel a lot of stuff is bullying."

For many students physical bullying is the face of bullying as a whole. With this mindset, students may deem social, verbal, and cyber forms of bullying as not being bullying at all. A male school staff member reported that students often have difficulty seeing experiences such as cyberbullying and rumor spreading as bullying activities, so he tends to not use the word cyberbullying when talking to students. He notes in this regard:

> I just don't think I've used that term, I bring up Facebook and text messaging just because I believe when students hear the word bullying I don't think they understand that it's not the same as it used to be. There are not kids in the hallways pushing up a kid against a locker and taking his lunch but that doesn't mean that isn't going to happen. Now there are students it's more of the social network or girls talking about one girl. They might not say anything to her, they don't touch her, they constantly talk about her. Spreading rumors, trying to get them to understand that is a form of bullying. I've had students that actually were straight A's and feel bullying is wrong and when you actually have this place where you are like you are participating in this and helping them see, it's eye opening for them.

Students that get straight A's and cause few problems at school also have difficulty understanding that spreading rumors is a form of bullying. Most of the battle for school staff is getting students to understand that social bullying (e.g., spreading rumors, talking about others, etc.)—whether online or face-to-face—is a form of bullying.

Another school staff member shared his perspective on the gray area where joking becomes bullying, an area in which students get lost:

> **Interviewer:** So they don't think of it as bullying?
>
> **Interviewee:** No they don't.
>
> **Interviewer:** They think of it as social interaction?
>
> **Interviewee:** Joking around sometimes and I've gone over that with students, like OK you can have your friend and you guys can talk about each other. But the thing you don't know, maybe your friend is not in the best mood that day and he didn't tell anyone and you are saying these things, and normally he's OK because he laughs. But you are not paying attention that he's not laughing at what you are saying about him today. That's a harder concept to get across.

Besides getting students to understand that social forms of bullying are actual bullying, school staff also have difficulty in explaining that bullying can be dependent on the individual context. What may be taken as joking one day, might be upsetting to a person the next.

A major difference between being face-to-face and Facebook is the perception of audience. When students are at school and talking to a group of their friends they see who is in front of them. On Facebook the audience is masked in a way that individuals may not always be thinking of who they may have added in the past that can see their posts and information. A female staff member indicated that this can become a problem when students add a lot of others as "friends":

> And I mean kids have 1,000 friends so one of them will forget that they are friends with someone and post something negative about them on their page and then they forget, oh yeah, I'm friends with them.

When students update their statuses or post messages on their closer friends' walls the rest of the people they have friended can see what they wrote. Students may inadvertently make a comment to their friend about a person at school that they are not friends with while at school, but may have forgotten that they had added them as a Facebook "friend" a long time ago. Another difference between face-to-face bullying and cyberbullying on Facebook that school staff cited was the repetitive nature to it:

> **Male Focus Group Participant:** In the face-to-face it eventually just disappears and is gone, but bullying online is just like oh look at this see and boom there it is, you can repeat it as many times as you want. I think the Internet gives almost more opportunity for people to become bullies because it's just so easy. You don't have to see that person...
>
> **Female Focus Group Participant:** And you need a lot less bravado to be a cyberbully. I think you need a certain level of confidence and bravado to be an actual bully. There is false confidence or whatever, but I don't think you need that necessarily [in cyberbullying].

These staff members indicated that the repetitive nature of social technology and the number of people that see what another might post is a contributing aspect to cyberbullying. Further, it seems easier for students to cyberbully than to be a physical in-person bully. Cyberbullies do not have to see their victims and do not necessarily need the confidence of an in-person bully. In an interview session a staff member spoke to this aspect as well:

> I have some cases where students will be in school everyday all day and never speak to each other. But on Facebook that's where they will, the term I use is keyboard gangsters because they get very tough behind the computer screen. But in the school they would never bother that person, they would never say anything about that person, ever. But on the Internet it's a totally different story.

Students may not speak to those other students they get into altercations with online face-to-face at school. When asked why this was, this staff member went on to speak to the appeal of being bold and having your friends there to back you up:

> I think they're more bold behind the keyboard. It's easier to get if you say something here in school to a person you know you are limited to the people who are there at that moment. Once you type it as a comment all your friends and maybe then some can all add on which kind of roots you on even more in doing that.

When students are face-to-face the things they say or do in a bullying manner are limited to those that are there at that particular moment. In contrast, online venues such as Facebook provide space for cyberbullying activity to occur at any time. This way the act can snowball into something larger with their friends adding to it with further comments. However, sometimes maliciousness is not the intended act. Being unable to see those you may be interacting with provides another problematic facet of confusion with social technology:

> **Male Interviewee:** … a lot of times emails, text messages can be taken the wrong way because there is no face-to-face visual emotion to it. Whereas even if the perceived bully says something face-to-face and then sees the reaction he or she might come back and say oh I'm sorry I didn't mean it like that. Whereas online none of that is there.

The lack of physical cues associated with social technology can create problems between individuals—friends even—as confusion can erupt as tone of voice and facial expressions are sometimes difficult to ascertain. What may seem like a joke in person may not be conveyed in the same manner online. School staff also reported that cyberbullying can affect victims in different ways, ranging from grades dropping, to being visibly upset at school, and to creating stress for them at home as a consequence of being bullied.

They spoke candidly regarding the kinds of cyberbullying that were most frequent in their schools. While pictures and videos directed at making fun of or bullying a fellow student had happened, written postings were the most common because they are the easiest to do, as they are the most available and most easily accessible. According to a male focus group participant, "It's far easier to post one or two words or a sentence than to post a picture or video." A common posting is through a status message:

> **Male Interviewee:** Yeah, because sometimes there will be an incident in the school and the person puts under a status—'These girls better be lucky we are at a private school. These girls better be lucky we go to [this school]' and they insinuate, won't say the names of the girls but everybody will know who they are talking about.

Even though staff members cited wall postings and status messages as the most common form of cyberbullying, a male interviewee also indicated that they had seen cyberbullying via pictures: "They may take a picture off another student's Facebook page and attach it to somebody else's body, doctor it or just alter the picture." With technology, using software such as Photoshop cyberbullying by means of purposes by downloading a photo from someone's Facebook page, and altering it in a derogatory manner, has been rather easy. Also, with cell phones having recording features video clips are also emerging as a way to cyberbully others:

> **Male Interviewee:** We had some videos. A student wrote a rap making fun of three other students. He wrote it and he had other students read the rap and he recorded it. He was never on tape or anything. But he was doing the posting. He admitted to writing the rap…it was really bad, bad stuff.

In this case a student wrote a rap about three other students, had other students rap it, and then posted it. Besides posting comments, pictures, and videos to Facebook a student could also utilize the newer Facebook features that involve creating groups and pages in cyberbullying activity. A male school staff member shared his experience:

> Students will make fake pages, for instance, Sluts of the City, and feature individuals, that's the type of stuff. No one will ever know for sure the person who makes the page, but that's the anonymity. Students would not be sitting out there saying those things out loud in school, they would never do those things where people would know what they were doing. A little bit of anonymity on the Internet that's when they do it.

When a page like this comes to the attention of school staff they work to find out who may have started it so it can be removed. As it may take a long time to figure out who may have been responsible for the site, as a group or page can be started anonymously, they often contact Facebook directly to remove the page:

> **Male Focus Group Participant:** We don't know, we had no idea [who started it]. When we found out we wrote Facebook requesting them to remove the page.
>
> **Focus Group Moderator:** OK. So this was a group of some kind?
>
> **Female Focus Group Participant:** It was mostly about the girls that were promiscuous. Kids were tagging them and saying they were promiscuous. You know all that.

The anonymity of the creator of a group or page can pose challenges for school staff who seek to find the perpetrator and remove the page for the victims. As the female focus group participant above indicated, gender plays a large role in cyberbullying at the middle and high school levels.

Gender and gender identity play large roles in growing up, and therefore play large roles in rumors, gossip, bullying, and cyberbullying phenomena. According to the school staff members taking part in the focus group session and interviews, a large amount of cyberbullying deals with issues of promiscuity, sexuality, and a variety of superficial things (e.g., clothes, physical attributes). Further, they stated many times and in many different ways that the cyberbullying tended to be focused most commonly on female victims. A male interviewee reported: "Females posting about females. Males posting about females. Two of them going back and forth arguing on Facebook while males about males is very rare." For the most part females cyberbully females and males cyberbully females, as well with cyberbullying between males being rare. A school staff member thought that this had to do with the difference between female students and males in dealing with conflict and altercations:

> **Male Interviewee:** It tends to be more the young ladies rather than the young men from what I observe here. They [young men] don't like someone or don't care for someone they just shut the person out, they'll avoid them. Young ladies don't avoid like the young men.

While the young men are more likely to avoid someone they do not like, females tend not to avoid those they do not like and sometimes end up in altercations. However, this staff member did indicate that some females handle these situations with a negative maturity:

> **Male Interviewee:** It's funny, I've seen some where the ladies respond negatively but I don't want to say this it's going to sound weird, negative but mature at the same time. So they respond, they may respond with profanity like shut the 'f' up they don't say anything back. They say something like you must not have a life if you are so worried about me, you must have nothing going on for you, you probably don't have anything better to do if you are so worried about me.

Even though this negative maturity can provoke the perpetrator and cause further escalation of cyberbullying activity, it reveals a confidence among some students where they do not allow cyberbullying to get to them. While they were clear that females were victimized more often, they were also clear that males were sometimes victimized when their sexuality came into question:

> **Female Focus Group Participant:** It'll be mainly boys that say things about girls but I don't hear much about boys. Well actually I take that back. This one incident was about a boy's sexuality but that was boys and girls that had posted something in the video or whatever. But I don't think as much. Mostly girls.

However, gender identity does not just affect males. As this female school staff focus group participant reveals, it can affect females as well:

> I've seen some of the Freshman, a couple of Freshmen that were suspended. It was because they were saying nasty things about two females that you know that have some sexual identity issues and an incident on a bus, at a game or something. It got all out of control with Facebook stuff and you know other students saying nasty bitches and what's up with that. Just so you know that's so disgusting, just and both these girls were so, so upset and first thing when they came to school, they were in my office crying about this. That's, I think, another obviously high thing in this age group, so much identity confusion going on.

Gender identity and identity in general are major topics with this age group, and social technology tools such as Facebook have the potential to magnify issues such as these. This school staff member talked about how freshmen were usually the perpetrators of the kind of cyberbullying incident noted above. A male school staff interviewee also spoke to age, noting that cyberbullying seemed to be more prevalent among younger students in high school:

> Yeah, it's definitely more freshmen and sophomore bullying. It decreases as they get older. One of the reasons I believe, we will do a review process twice a year and after the review process our schools a little bit stronger, I mean the school's a little bit smaller…so anyone who makes it to junior or senior year assuming they started out as freshman those are people making better decisions. By the time you get to senior year usually they are more focused on finishing up and going to college as opposed to all the social stuff. By the time they are seniors because they are so focused. Which is just natural maturation, we hope that it is. It is definitely more lower classmen than upper classmen to the point where if it does happen in upper classmen you try your hardest to put a trip on them, like you are a senior. I don't have these conversations with seniors, why are you even in my office for something like this. I don't see seniors in my office a lot until the second week of April when they start getting antsy, time to leave.

As a private school, the school had more leeway when it came to punishing students for cyberbullying activity; students and parents had agreed to abide by their honor code in this regard. This is not to say that this school just expelled students easily. There was an understanding that sometimes students did not understand what they were doing or thought they were doing the right thing when coming to the defense of a friend. In doing so they found themselves involved in the reciprocal nature of cyberbullying:

> **Male Interviewee**: We've had students that are these great students at our school who may not necessarily have anything to do with the situation who when they see something bad happening, they are trying to prevent it. They've come to us, they are amazing. That's one way of knowing that a person may be involved and then realize this is going too far and they'll come and they'll admit they did. They'll admit their part which I think shows a little bit of maturity because we respect [that].

Even though students may not be involved with the particular situation or got involved to defend a friend, they might see it spiraling out of control and contact staff. School staff were also aware of the complexity of relationships potentially involved in cyberbullying activity:

> **Male Interviewee:** …it's so hard to know the absolute origin. I've said that to students who are sophomores in high school and they'll say something like we were in prep school together—hold on you mean 7th grade, 8th grade. So hold on you mean you are going back to 7th grade and you are in 10th grade.

In some cyberbullying cases, animosity between students can begin in middle school and emerge later on. While situations such as these can be the case, school staff also spoke about the times when cyberbullying activity was more likely to take place. Sometimes it felt like it was rather random in nature, as the following observation indicates:

> **Male Interviewee:** ...it always comes in groups. I never understood it—you could get three or four incidents that are not related at all within a week. Never hear anything for three months and then you get three or four more incidents that are not related within a week.

This school staff member thinking about it further narrowed it down a bit:

> **Male Interviewee:** Usually and I'm becoming better at predicting busier times. Before Christmas break, before Easter break, four day weekends, the longer weekends that's when we usually have issues.
>
> **Interviewer:** Before or after?
>
> **Male Interviewee:** Right before. Sometimes after something happens during the break and it comes back to school.
>
> **Interviewer:** I'm surprised it happens before I thought it would be more likely to happen after.
>
> **Male Interviewee:** Well the reason it happens before, a theory of course, the reason we have it before is like I say, we are a pretty good school and you can talk to any students at random they think school is cool. Sometimes our students may not necessarily have a good situation outside the school. So those long breaks are not always something they are looking forward to because they are not going to come in and see all of their friends every day. It's a break from routine. Break to routine is extremely detrimental—it's bad. And a good way you know if you are going to miss a place, no matter where it is on vacation or if you have to move, some people in general tend to make this place negative so it's not as bad when you have to move away. That's why the longer breaks I'm prepared to have to be busy.

For students without a good situation outside of school the break from routine when school holidays come around make them act out. Since they enjoy coming to school and do not want to miss it, they act out negatively to make themselves feel like they will miss it less. School staff reflected that it was their job to uphold the rules, protocol, and policies of the school while being understanding of student motivation and background.

Chapter Summary

Students and staff indicated that Facebook was not the problem, but rather it was how social networks were used (e.g., for cyberbullying activity) that created problems. Cyberbullying activity can lead to arguing in class or even physical altercations. It can be perpetrated by anyone as it does not require physical strength making the potential perpetrator pool larger than those that may become a physical bully. Students and staff perceived that cyberbullies tended to be female and focus on victimization of female students. In some cases males participated in cyberbullying females and males were victimized when their sexuality was questioned. Students and staff both indicated that age played a role in cyberbullying activity with younger students (e.g., Freshmen, Sophomores) more likely to be involved than their older counterparts. Both groups agreed that cyberbullying was quite serious as it tends to spread quickly to a large group of people and never fully goes away.

Students and staff disagreed over the question of what a "friend" was. Staff focused on knowing people and knowing people in a genuine fashion in order to consider them a friend. These friends are also their "friends" on Facebook. Students made no distinction between those kinds of friends and "friends." Further, students indicated that they often added people they knew to their Facebook accounts as "friends," but that they were far less picky about adding individuals. If students met an individual through a friend, at an event, or knew someone from school they added them. Adults that reflected that their Facebook "friends" were also people they considered to be genuine friends.

A difference between students and staff was also apparent in how cyberbullying was defined. School staff members were more aware that social and verbal bullying via gossip and rumors often contributed to cyberbullying. While students did speak about these different components in the focus group sessions, the connection was not always clear for them. In many cases students indicated that cyberbullying was "bullying through the Internet" but had difficulty explaining further what it was. One student explained that they do not even use the term cyberbullying, and instead just think of everything (e.g., gossip, rumors, talking about others) together.

CHAPTER 10

Approaches to Combatting Cyberbullying in School

> "I never put myself on the same level as an actual detective, but there is a lot of detective work when my office is here the incident that happens in the classroom. I'm not there, there are no physical clues or anything so all you have to go on is what people say."—School staff member

During interviews and the focus group session school staff members spent time explaining their school policies, protocols, and approaches to combatting cyberbullying behavior in their schools.

SCHOOL POLICIES, PROCESSES, AND PROTOCOLS

School staff members reported that their schools had various policies regarding cell phone and Facebook use in place. Participants indicated that cell phones were not allowed in school, but that students found ways to use them. One staff member indicated that students even texted in their sweatshirt pouches during class. However, if students were caught using their cell phones they had them taken away, and there was a demanding process to get them back:

> **Male Interviewee:** Once they undergo a process where the parent or guardian must call and set up an appointment. They come in we sit down go over the policy procedures. I give them a release form and they pay a $25 fine and then they get their phone back.

Once caught using their cell phones when forbidden, students must go home to tell their parent or guardian that they had used their cell phone during school. At that point the parent or guardian must call the school, review the cell phone policy, and pay the monetary fine due before the student is allowed to have their phone back. School staff members commented that sometimes the parents were the ones contacting their children during class.

> **Female Focus Group Participant 1:** The interesting thing is the parents know this policy, but they'll send texts to their kids.
>
> **Female Focus Group Participant 2:** Yeah. (Laughter)
>
> **Female Focus Group Participant 1:** So it's kind of hard to take the cell phone away when the parent is actually interacting with them. It's like well they are in class right now. We have parents text them like a joke. I'm like, are you serious, they are sitting in biology and they need a joke. I think they need to pay attention to biology but (Laughter). So a lot of times a teacher will try to discipline them and will look at what the last couple of text messages were and they'll find it's a parent or something. I just find that really, really odd. What if I need to get a hold of my kid, well how about calling the main office and we can find them anywhere they are in the building. I know it's kind of old-fashioned but they are not supposed to have it in class because it's such a huge distraction.

Parents want to be able to get a hold if their children while they are away from them, but some parents abuse the ability to have that connection by contacting their child during class. As this school staff member indicated, the information that the parents are texting to the student may not even be of essential nature—it may be a joke or other information that could wait until after school. Schools also restricted students from using Facebook during school hours. However, as with cell phones, students found clever ways to use Facebook while at school:

> **Female Focus Group Participant:** They are not really supposed to. Do they? Of course they do, they access it absolutely yes.

> **Male Focus Group Participant:** We do have, a like, I don't know if Firewall is the right word for it, but there's tunnels they use.
>
> **Female Focus Group Participant:** Well they can easily get around it because if somebody posts something on your Wall and it's sent to Yahoo or Hotmail you can get right on because it will say click the link and you're in. So it's there's a block but it's really…
>
> **Male Focus Group Participant:** Yes, it's easy to overcome it. They can easily, they get around it.

Students find ways to access Facebook even though it is a blocked site and inaccessible by going to the website itself. School staff members reported that students were allowed to access their emails during lunch or breaks in computer class. However, it is during this period of time where students can use notifications from Facebook to their email to access the site. Like the male focus group participant mentioned above, another school staff member also reported the use of websites to tunnel under the school's firewall system:

> **Male Interviewee:** Yeah, there are ways we have it blocked so they can't access it. It's amazing how ingenious our students can get. Actually saw a student on Facebook one time and I wasn't even upset, I wanted to know how he got on. He quickly clicked off when he saw me looking at his screen. I didn't want to know who was there I just wanted to know how he did it. I found out from him that there was a place out there that you can go to and type on a website and it literally tunnels under our firewall to get to the website we don't give access to.

Growing up with an understanding of technology and how things work gives teenagers a special knowledge of workarounds. By Googling a phrase such as "how to get on Facebook at school" students can start digging through information to help them achieve their goal. As many phones require data plans they have access to the Internet, this gives students access to Facebook at any time, any place—including school:

> **Male Interviewee:** Yeah well, at lunch time when we say it is not allowed it still happens. I've had, it's a whole another conversation cell phones, that's another way to get on Facebook during the school day. What the students don't understand is I'm really close to a lot of my former students and sometimes they are like hey, so and so updated their Facebook status, because they are friends with a former student, I'm like really?

Even though the school had a cell phone policy where students were not to use them during the school day, many students still gambled that they would not be caught in order to be able to update their status. As this school staff member reported, prior students with whom they are friends may become informants on current student behavior.

When asked how they found out about cyberbullying activity, school staff members indicated that often students involved in the situation had low privacy settings, but that they mostly approached school staff for help:

> **Female Focus Group Participant:** It might be a matter of better of them not putting in securities, but it's also other students who will come to us and say this is what this person posted. So, that kid can pull up the other kid's Facebook page so then you can see that stuff.

When students are involved in cyberbullying activity on Facebook and have low privacy settings, school staff can investigate the situation by going to that student's page to see what has been posted. When students come to school staff for help they may also pull up information from their account that shows the activity in question. A female school staff member reported that students were rather forthcoming regarding cyberbullying:

> I mean they are usually pretty open about coming to us—it seems like us or the Dean of Students. They are usually not afraid to speak up and come talk to us if there's something like that going on.

While staff reported that students felt comfortable with school staff and were not afraid to come to them for help, sometimes it was friends of those involved in cyberbullying activity that came to them instead:

> **Female Focus Group Participant:** I think most students, even if it's not the kid's involved will have a friend come and say something to us or they are pretty open about coming to us.

Staff members get involved in cyberbullying incidents when some of those involved or friends of those involved come forward. However, their involvement does not stop at listening to student stories. It extends into gathering information, doing some detective work, collecting evidence, referring cases to a higher school entity, and for those higher entities to determine punishment.

At one school a guidance teacher spoke of the integral relationship between the school's staff—especially the teachers and the guidance counselors:

> **Female Focus Group Participant:** If they [teachers] see a student that's upset or crying or whatever they will usually send them up here [to the Guidance Office]. We have a really good relationship with the staff, I think, with the teachers and they are really quick to send the kid that's upset or anything up here.

As classrooms are the place where students spend most of their time, teachers are at the front line in discovering cyberbullying behavior. As students spend time with their guidance counselors they may feel more comfortable in sharing things with them. When teachers send students to the guidance office because they are upset due to bullying and cyberbullying activity they generally worked with their victimized students to gain an understanding of the situation:

> **Focus Group Moderator:** And then what's your next step? How do you approach these kinds of issues?

> **Male Focus Group Participant:** I talk to the student and I ask them to give me any information they know about it and then just look into it.
>
> **Female Focus Group Participant:** I usually take them to the Dean of Discipline, the Assistant Dean of Discipline, because they are the ones that can really. We don't issue any discipline for the kids, they do. So if we see something like that we probably would give it to them and they would go to the Principal and it would go off from there.

If guidance counselors determine that the situation is serious, they send the student to meet with the Dean of Students. A male guidance counselor reported that it was difficult for them and out of their scope to further investigate the cyberbullying activity:

> I mean it is hard to know how much is going on. I know a couple of cases and one they took down the page. I never really interviewed any of the—I didn't know any of the people actually targeted, but I did talk to some of the friends and you know I haven't heard anything else from them.

Without the time and skills needed to investigate cyberbullying to its fullest extent and lacking the punitive power to reprimand individuals, the students end up spending time meeting with the Dean. When it came to cyberbullying activity, the Dean likened the work of finding out what really happened in the situation to the work that a detective might encounter:

> I never put myself on the same level as an actual detective, but there is a lot of detective work when my office is here the incident that happens in the classroom. I'm not there, there are no physical clues or anything so all you have to go on is what people say.

Armed with information from teachers and guidance counselors, the Dean begins to put the pieces of the situation together. However, in order to gain a more comprehensive understanding of the situation that occurred they also talk to the students involved. When the Dean met with students he explained how he often asked them to see the cyberbullying activity by pulling up the incident on their account:

> It's usually connected with an incident and they never just let me see [it all], like I said I maybe opening a whole 'nother can of worms…I print it out or take a page shot which is easy.

By meeting with students and having them pull up the incidents on their accounts it allowed him to gather evidence to make a decision on how to further handle the situation. He was clear in that he only wanted to see information directly to the incident in question and not the rest of the student's account or their other interactions as that would be "opening a whole 'nother can of worms" by seeing things about students he does not want to see. The Dean went on to describe how he went about talking to students when they had an altercation with one another, and eventually arranged a meeting with all involved:

> Take the example of the young ladies who got into a conflict and it was a young man pulling her strings and none of them was aware of how that worked so I explained that to them. Before I get them together I prepare them and I just ask them very basic questions like please name for me everything that she did or said that you know for a fact that she did or said. That you saw her or heard her say that affected you. Most of the time they don't have anything so I'm like so you are going off on what you heard. I'm like you might be right maybe she did, maybe she didn't, you don't know that. Get them to focus on facts, get them to focus on even if we know this person said something bad about them what bearing does this have on your future success. If it's none, why do you really care. I just say it that much slower when I'm talking because I really want it to sink in. I tell them, it'll only be a small amount of people who really you hold who their pain means something to you.

By getting students together and allowing them the opportunity to get an understanding of the situation from the other person's perspective, it gives those involved the chance to learn and move on. The Dean also gives advice from an adult perspective to students involved by telling them to focus on the facts, but even if it comes out that someone did say something about you as a fact that you should consider the source and how much that person, and what they say, actually means to you. However, the situation is not always easy to figure out for the Dean. Many times the investigation leads the Dean to having to sort through blame and excuses:

> They blame someone else, even after I've been through the process, oh yeah my cousin has my password, my sister. I usually give them the look, without really saying anything, you really think I started doing this today? (Laughs) I say to them you know we all mess up. We all make mistakes and it's so much easier to respect someone who admits and can fess up to their mistakes.

Students will sometimes blame the cyberbullying activity on another person that they indicate has the password to their account. The Dean indicated that this was rare and was much more likely to end up being the student in question committing the activity they blamed on the "mysterious other" individual (e.g., cousin, sister) who had their password. He said that he had developed a tactic in questioning where he asked them about sharing their passwords before getting to why he was meeting with the student:

> I would bring [the student] in and start a casual conversation with [them] and ask… hey are you on Facebook? Just say like do you share your Facebook page with anyone else. The answer's always no. So, you say you don't share your password with your friends, right? They say no. So, I'll say all that stuff on Facebook that you posted, that would have to be you right and they say yeah and are you sure and they say yeah. So, well can you explain this? Once I get it out of the way that they are the only possible person that could have done it cause it's the anonymity of it. It's a little bit of squirming and everything then you might find out more details. Maybe that person did say something about them before, maybe even on Facebook. Then show me that part you find out some other details.

By starting out with asking students whether or not they share their Facebook passwords it later eliminates the credibility in students using that as an excuse. When this aspect can be skipped it leaves more opportunity to get more details and an even fuller understanding of what happened from multiple points of view. Blaming others for the cyberbullying activity was not the only obstacle to investigation encountered by school staff. The Dean also explained that there were times when students outright lied:

> It's very futile with me, some people will, they will lie. I just had this student on videotape, showed it to her and she continued to deny it with the video playing. Some people (laughs), that situation didn't go too well. I had her on video doing the thing that she denied, clear, no doubt whatsoever. She continued to deny it to me and her mother. The mother pretty much flipped her top when she saw the video. She couldn't understand, I never thought a student could go that far. When you don't want to get into trouble you say what you think works.

When confronted with what they have done, students may try saying anything to get out of being in trouble. Understanding this, school staff work to collect as much independent evidence and information about the situation as possible and take that, along with the student's willingness to come forward, into their decisions regarding punishment.

The Dean reported that it highly depended on the situation as to how those involved in the cyberbullying activity were punished:

> Since most of them are just minor…it can be something like talking to with the parent contact and [saying] you guys can have no contact, first talking to each other, no teasing, no glares, no anything what so ever.

The first step was to talk to the students, but then to get the parents involved to discuss the situation with the Dean of Students and the Principal. As part of the sanction to be able to remain at the school students had to agree to have no negative contact with each other. If it reoccurs or is a more severe incident students undergo further punishment as they may be suspended, asked to leave, or expelled.

School staff who participated in the focus group session shared an experience that had occurred in their school where some students were suspended and others were expelled:

> **Female Focus Group Participant 1:** There was the incident that happened not too long ago. It was a video that was actually shot on a cell phone in front of our school and kids talking just craziness about other kids and swearing. So, a couple of them were, a couple were my students and they were, I mean they had done past discipline things. So, the ones that were already on shaky ground, they were expelled. So, there were a couple other ones that were involved, but they probably got a suspension of a couple days.

> **Female Focus Group Participant 2:** I think the ones that I know that got suspended were maybe in the video, they weren't the main, they didn't post, they didn't do as much of the, you know talking. They were in it and I think it more hinged on what they had done in the past.

According to these staff members both those that have had prior disciplinary problems at school and those that play a main role in the cyberbullying activity are at risk of being expelled. They indicated that it was necessary to take incidents such as these seriously to keep the school safe for their students as a whole. The Dean explained that students that, depending on the situation, are asked to leave the school have the option to leave via withdrawal or expulsion:

> We have this thing where we say withdrawn, which is very similar, but a student withdrawn has the chance to come back maybe at a future date, if you are expelled that's it. That's the only difference. Either way you are leaving then and there, but you have the chance of coming back.

Many students who are offered the chance to leave by the withdrawal method do so as it gives them a possibility of returning to the school at some point during their high school careers. This school was private and had more power than a public school would to create policy, protocol, and sanctions:

> **Female Focus Group Participant:** Well we have a different luxury than other schools—we can just get rid of them. I don't know if that is really helping the problem. We are removing them from here, but that doesn't mean we are removing them from online. Just because they are gone doesn't mean they are really gone.

Being a private school gives school staff advantages in having the power to easily, within reason, to ask students to leave or expel them. While this helps school staff to keep the school environment safe, it does not mean that students that leave do not have contact with students currently enrolled there. This could lead to further problems with students being cyberbullied by students no longer enrolled there.

School staff that participated in focus group and interview sessions discussed approaches and tactics they used to prevent cyberbullying from happening now or in the future. A female guidance counselor spoke about the importance of having cyberbullying perpetrators and victims get together to discuss what happened and get to know one another better:

> I think it could be because they are never face-to-face on Facebook so when you actually sit down with the other person I think that might change their mind. Like oh, I'm really saying something about an actual person you know where they are like they might not say it to their face or in front of other students, where they maybe think twice about doing it again.

This school staff member thought that the facelessness and the boldness one gets from not being face-to-face with a person contributes to cyberbullying activity. By getting them together to talk in a mediation approach cyberbullying perpetrators can see the pain they cause their victims. Also, it gives students who may think they are really different—and pick on those differences—to understand one another better, which was likely to reduce further cyberbullying perpetration. The Dean of Students that was interviewed also indicated he liked to talk to students, and gave an example of how he engaged the transfer students specifically:

> I always personally speak to the transfer students. Welcome them to the school, give them an idea how we do things here. Give them different examples, situations they may encounter for being in high school, how would they deal with it, why would they do it that way. Sort of give them advice, the best way to deal with the situation in order to prevent other things from happening. Also we have the summer program for incoming ninth graders. Every year I have always spoken to them, always try to give them the hints for what to expect from high school. Things to stay away from, things to gravitate towards. I'm very, very big on the preventative.

By alerting new students about the school's expectations regarding school and out-of- school interactions it gives these student an understanding of acceptable behavior. Also, due to some students being unaware of actions that constitute cyberbullying, it would be important to give new students actual illustrative examples of cyberbullying and what to do if it would happen to them. This would give students that are new to the school a solid foundation for staying out of trouble and where to seek if they find themselves in trouble.

School staff members also take proactive approaches to finding cyberbullying activity. One way that was mentioned was by checking YouTube for videos making fun of others:

> **Male Focus Group Participant:** … maybe check you know like YouTube you know every once in a while and then they will type in [the school name] just to see what's out there. But I don't know if there is someone that will regularly check certain people. I've even done that myself, looked at YouTube. I don't look at Facebook much.

While no one is assigned to do this and staff did not do this on a regular basis, they sometimes used the search feature of YouTube to proactively find potential videos that would be harmful to students in their school. Even though students indicated that staff tried to create fake profiles to monitor their interactions, school staff indicated that they did not do that and thought it was a bad idea:

> **Male Interviewee:** I figured the bad would outweigh the good that would come out of that. The way we look at things is, if I made a fake Facebook page and I became friends with students and I had knowledge of these things and couldn't do anything about it I am liable. I have possibility of the knowledge of these things that's why we try to be more proactive and try to wait until things come to us also because we were pretty sure there are some. Even if there is no bullying there are things on their Facebook page that they shouldn't be putting out there.

For much the same reason that staff did not accept friendship requests of current students, staff also did not create fake profiles to monitor student interactions and activity on Facebook. Seeing things that students might post not only changes the way they might perceive them, but also creates a situation where they may know of something that is happening (e.g., a party) and not have the power to do anything while at the same time knowing creates a liability. Besides individual school staff actions against cyberbullying, the school also put tactics into place to reduce student altercations. During a focus group session a school staff member explained that they had implemented a block schedule:

> **Female Focus Group Participant:** A days and B days. So A days is 4 classes. B days is 4 classes. Rotates every other day. So it's definitely, definitely taken that fighting or pushing or shoving down quite a bit because there is not as big of an opportunity to interface in the hall way. I mean like it's not like we ever really had that much of that issue. Plus we've shortened our lunch hours. They used to be like a 50 some minutes lunch hour – they were a full hour long and now they are 30 minutes. So, it gives them a little bit less time. They can eat in that amount of time and they are just sitting and that's when a lot of the problems happen. Sitting idle waiting for whatever to happen.

By implementing a block schedule the school took an active measure to decrease the number of times students switch classes and see each other in the hallway, as well as the amount of time allowed to eat lunch. The decrease in how often and how long students see each other has potential to decrease the number of altercations that take place on school grounds. However, online cyberbullying activity can still take place after school or during holidays.

The school staff members that participated in the focus group and interview sections also talked about the school's student handbooks and the role they played:

> **Male Focus Group Participant:** I have our harassment policy and this is the parent guardian student handbook. Sort of says if behavior either physical, verbal or virtual that hinders the learning teaching environment that can be interpreted as threatening to others will not be tolerated.

This participant worked in a private school and indicated that the student handbook which the school had created was very important. It was seen as a cornerstone of power as it held students to a level of conduct, both in school and outside of school, where actions that threatened the learning environment and other students would not be tolerated. The Dean of Students elaborated on this policy:

> We say all these things on Facebook and it is no different if you say it here. Just like we told them that if you get into a verbal altercation or physical altercation in [the mall] it's no different if it happened here, it is treated the same way. That's because we feel you are always representing our school. So that that's a tough mission and sometimes parents [don't agree]. I do have conversations with the parents, like I had a parent who was an educator at a public school and her son was suspended for some things he said on Facebook. And she could not understand, like this did not happen at school. I like to think about it as that when things like this happen they come into school, we don't want all this to come to school. This is our preventative, we never want a student out of school but we much rather have them out for a day or two as opposed to something bad happens and now he has to be expelled. You have to choose the lesser of two evils.

As part of the school's mission they adopted they believe that as a student you are a representative of the school when you are outside of school. This makes it easier for the school to get involved in situations that their students are involved in outside of school, whether at the mall or virtually on Facebook. School staff also reflected on the need for a school-wide prevention program or curriculum, which they did not have.

NEED FOR PREVENTION PROGRAMS

Some individual staff members did cyberbullying prevention activities with students, but those that participated in focus group and interview sessions indicated that they would like to see a more school-wide prevention program effort. School staff mentioned that the prevention program should feature basic education regarding social technology use—especially Facebook privacy settings and measures to be taken toward being safe on the Internet. A school staff member said that he knew that students understand how to access Facebook, but was not sure if they were aware of the latest ways to protect themselves when utilizing the site. Even if they had an understanding of the privacy settings, there were other issues:

> **Male Interviewee:** A normal teenager in my opinion tends to be a know it all and they figure they have control of those privacy settings. They have control of what they put out there and they do to a certain extent. A young man who was involved in one of our more serious Facebook incidents, who is no longer here, I told him you understand how mean this is and how wrong it is to do something like that. And he proceeded to tell me that it's private and I said, but I know about it. You didn't mean for me to read this here did you and he said no. So, how private is it if you didn't mean me to see it, I saw it. Let's assume that I can't see it. You have 500 people in your friends list. Pretty sure you don't know half of the 500 people I said and they have friends so we really don't know how many people actually saw what you posted. But we can guarantee at least 500 have access to it. Then the wheels started to turn in those one-on-one conversations.

The concept of privacy is one that must be further discussed with students as it is more than just a matter of privacy settings. Instead it encompasses both the settings and thinking clearly about what you decide to post. Using higher privacy settings was one aspect mentioned, but they also called for a way to get students to think about the items they post. Generally it was not a good idea to post information regarding how students can be contacted or found:

> **Female Focus Group Participant:** I think they need, I think what I was trying to get at too was how much stuff are you putting out there. Like you have your cell phone number on Facebook, would you just walk up to some random stranger at the mall and say here is my cell phone number. That's what I said when I was in class—you don't do stuff like that. Here's my address, here's my cell phone number…someone could look and find oh this girl lives at this address and her parents aren't at home at such and such time and then they just target her and get over there. So, I think that is not even so much cyber, I mean I think they are aware of the cyberbullying, but I think they are not aware of how much stuff they are putting out there and how at risk they are making themselves.

According to this participant students are sometimes unaware of the ramifications having information, like their phone number and address, out there can lead to. Therefore, it would be important to include this as a topic in a potential prevention program. School staff thought that to get the point across it was important to give noteworthy examples about consequences of cyberbullying activity:

> **Female Focus Group Participant:** And I think here they realize it goes quickly—that so and so was expelled for something on Facebook. And I think they could easily learn oh I better be careful what I put out there … teenagers don't even know what they are going to do tomorrow let alone what they are entering.

School staff viewed students as being short-sided and living in the now by posting things and not thinking about how it would affect them or the people they are posting about. Staff thought that providing actual examples would make the importance of the program resonate with students. Another school staff member said it might be a good idea to include consequences related to things in their futures:

> **Female Focus Group Participant:** Maybe the effect something has had on just later on in life. Like umm OK so I tried to get into this college and all this college had to do was go type my name in Facebook and there is all this underage drinking pictures. And then they got a rejection letter or people that have gotten fired from their jobs for posting dumb things like I hate my job, I hate work, my boss is an idiot, your boss is your friend and stuff like that.

By showing students what they do now can affect their futures, like college acceptances and employment opportunities, it may divert students from participating in cyberbullying or posting inappropriate things. One school staff member had a vision of what such a program would look like:

> **Male Interviewee:** Definitely an orientation program and maybe refreshers every couple of months. Just as human beings we are not always the best at remembering information that we hear one time. So, sometimes we have this faulty expectation I told you this, why did you do this. But we talked in September and it's now April so of course it's totally out of their mind.
>
> **Interviewer:** What would those refreshers look like? Like a hand-out or a?
>
> **Male Interviewee:** Hand-out maybe going over things in classroom settings. Maybe not large group but classroom setting. I'm big on discussions so asking them questions, and then coming up have students come up with solutions, which they will have no problems with. I think that's what would be useful.

This staff member thought that an orientation program every year with follow-up refreshers would be most appropriate, as it would keep the topic fresh in students' minds. These sessions, while focusing on the topics discussed above, would be best done in a classroom setting where discussions and case studies with students coming up with solutions would be featured.

OTHER RELATED THOUGHTS

There were various comments made throughout the focus group and interview sessions that were related to their students and social technology use, but which did not fit into the themes and topics discussed above. While the focus of the interviews and focus group sessions were cyberbullying, school staff spoke very highly of their students:

> **Male Interviewee:** I think sometimes, I believe sometimes adults in general confuse teenagers immaturity and not fully acknowledge how bright how brilliant they are. But it's sometimes hard to understand just because the immaturity or the silly mistakes bad decisions, I think I've encountered some of the most brilliant young men and women, people ever. There is this one young man, he will get bored in class he will doodle because he likes science, he will doodle DNA code. Who does that? (Laughs) He loves Science, at the same time failed Science even though he loved it with a passion knew everything that was going on in class, fully understood but for some reason did not quite do the work, but he was on another level. Might not have multiple students like that but adults can't always see because of all the other stuff that get in the way.

When talking about cyberbullying adults may get a bad impression of youth. However, as this staff member mentioned, teenagers may make silly mistakes or bad decisions from time to time, but still have amazing characteristics that make them stand out. This school staff member worked at a private school and spoke about how even though they had more latitude to create policy and have students leave the facility if they did not abide by the set policies, that it was more about appropriate expectations:

> **Male Interviewee:** I tell them and people don't believe me when I say this. There is no difference as far as the actual student here or in the public schools. They come from the same neighborhoods. Sometimes they might be in the same family. There's no difference—it's like we have different, we're not pulling from a different pool but the simple fact is teenagers are the same as every other adult human being. We for the most part, will live up to the expectations that we have to. I know for a fact that I would speed a lot more if I was not at risk of getting a ticket or having to deal with the consequences that came with that. Students will, people always test those limits. When they know where those limits are they will most of the time stay within them. But it's the same kids, it's the same kids.

While school staff from public schools think that private schools have a different population, and therefore have fewer problems, this school staff member indicates that this is not actually the case. Many of their students come from the very same neighborhoods and families as those that attend the local public schools. Instead this school staff member believes that it has more to do with how much work is expected of the students, the limits set on student conduct, and how those limits are enforced.

Parental influence and supportiveness were also brought up in focus group and interview sessions alike. One school staff member indicated that for the most part they had supportive parents:

> **Male Interviewee:** I believe the overall majority of our parents are great. You can't help the small percentage that you wonder who allowed you to be a parent. But the overall majority they are outstanding and supportive in every way.

Even though they had supportive parents for the most part, they also had a few parents that were not supportive and did not teach their child the behavior and language differences between different environments (e.g., home and school).

Chapter Summary

Staff reported a number of policies, processes, protocols, and strategies that their schools were utilizing to combat cyberbullying. These included policies regarding cell phones and Facebook, investigation practices, and sanctions for perpetrating cyberbullying. Most interesting was the discontinuity between students and staff regarding how students deal with cyberbullying. While school staff spoke highly of their protocol and how students were likely to utilize them for help when it came to victimization from cyberbullying, this same protocol that made students look elsewhere for help. In many of the focus group sessions students indicated that they would not go to their teachers if they were cyberbullied. One student stated that he did not trust his teachers. Students revealed that this mistrust and lack of willingness to go to school staff stemmed from reporting requirements (of shared items), and this sharing of content sometimes made things worse (e.g., them becoming a "snitch"). Instead students utilized other strategies for dealing with cyberbullying such as ignoring it, confronting the perpetrator or backing up friends. If it was a serious situation students said they would tell someone but they were more likely to go to their parents, older siblings, or friends before informing teachers and school staff.

CHAPTER 11

Final Remarks

> "I just don't think I've used that term, I bring up Facebook and text messaging just because I believe when students hear the word bullying I don't think they understand that it's not the same as it used to be. There are not kids in the hallways pushing up a kid against a locker and taking his lunch but that doesn't mean that isn't going to happen. Now there are students it's more of the social network or girls talking about one girl. They might not say anything to her, they don't touch her, they constantly talk about her. Spreading rumors, trying to get them to understand that is a form of bullying. I've had students that actually were straight A's and feel bullying is wrong and when you actually have this place where you are like you are participating in this and helping them see, it's eye opening for them."—Male school staff member

The quantitative and qualitative findings of this study provided insight into the cyberbullying phenomenon. This chapter will begin by examining the research questions and how they connect to the literature and study findings. After the research questions are explored, limitations of this study are acknowledged and the significance of the findings are discussed. The chapter concludes with final remarks and the identification of avenues for future research.

INTERPRETATION OF FINDINGS

This section will focus on reviewing the instant research questions relative to the literature and the study results. This study was guided by the following research questions:

Quantitative	1. How frequently do middle and high school students engage in cyberbullying behaviors?
	2. Which demographic variables (i.e., gender, age, race, etc.) describe cyberbullying activity for middle and high school students?
	3. How does social technology cyberbullying relate to risky behaviors and feelings of school safety for middle and high school students?
Qualitative (Central)	4. What is social technology cyberbullying for middle and high school students?
Qualitative (Sub questions)	4a. How do students define cyberbullying?
	4b. What experiences have they had with cyberbullying activity?
	4c. Where does cyberbullying take place?
	4d. How has cyberbullying impacted their peer interactions?
	4e. How has cyberbullying activity impacted their perceptions of their school environment?
	4f. How has cyberbullying activity impacted their participation in risky behaviors?
Mixed Methods	5. To what extent and in what ways do qualitative data collection (i.e., focus groups and open-ended survey questions) among middle and high school students serve to contribute to a more comprehensive understanding of social technology use and cyberbullying for middle and high school students?

Subsequent sections will discuss the frequency of cyberbullying activity, demographic descriptors (e.g., race, gender, age) associated with cyberbullying engagement, and the connection between cyberbullying and engagement in risky behaviors and the relationship between school safety and cyberbullying. The discussion of these areas is followed by an interpretation of student perceptions related to cyberbullying issues. This section concludes with a reflection on how the quantitative and qualitative pieces of this study worked together to create a more comprehensive understanding of the complex phenomenon known as cyberbullying.

Frequency of Cyberbullying

Researchers have reported cyberbullying victimization rates ranging from 11% (Kowalski & Limber, 2007) of participating students being cyberbullied over the past few months to 72% (Juvonen & Gross, 2008) reporting at least one online incident of bullying in that time period. The findings from this concurred as just over 11% of the participating students reported being victimized by some form of cyberbullying over the past year. Among this 11% of students reporting some degree of victimization, 1.4% indicated that victimization occurred daily, 1.9% a few times per week, 2.5% a few times per month, and 5.3% a few times per year. These findings are lower than those of Kowalski and Limber (2007) who cited 11% over a few month period; this study shows that 5.8% reported cyberbullying taking place between a few times per month and daily. The differences in these findings could be related to a different timeframe being used as well as the way cyberbullying may have been defined on the survey instrument.

This study indicated that 11% of students who took the survey reported being victimized by a cyberbullying act within the span of a year. While 11% may not seem like a large percentage, given the number of student respondents (n=3,403) this means that hundreds of students reported regular cyberbullying victimization. More alarming was the fact that some students reported an intense victimization pattern, with 1.4% of the students reporting victimization daily and 1.9% weekly. While students who participated in focus groups did not indicate that they had been intensely victimized, they nonetheless spoke poignantly about the impact cyberbullying has on its victims based on what they heard from other students. Cyberbullying can make teenagers feel sad, depressed, and anxious about attending school. While on school grounds cyberbullying acts can manifest in verbal and physical confrontations. These instances of confrontation can lower the student's self-esteem, their comfort in remaining a student at that particular school, or become a detriment to their physical safety.

Prior literature in the field indicates that between 4% (Kowalski and Limber, 2007) and 14.5% (Li, 2007) of students report committing cyberbullying acts over a few months' timeframe. In this study a majority of students (80.4%) reported never perpetrating an act of cyberbullying. However, 7.4% of students reported cyberbullying others at least a few times per month. These findings are rather consistent with the literature, and fall between the range that current literature depicts as stated above. This study shows that the perpetration of cyberbullying acts is more common than victimization, suggesting that a small number of victims may be disproportionately targeted by bullies in a cumulative or "piling-on" effect. The qualitative data collected in this study indicated a reciprocal nature to cyberbullying behavior (i.e., the victim may retaliate and become the perpetrator). The quantitative data showed that cyberbullying victims and perpetrators have a number of co-existing variables, including drug usage, engagement with violence, and engagement in traditional bullying. Given the qualitative and quantitative data regarding the reciprocal nature of the phenomenon and the existence of correlates to cyberbullying, it is important to investigate the act in full extent. Focusing on the act in this manner will provide perpetrators, victims, and witnesses with viable options for help when cyberbullying situations emerge.

Demographic Descriptors

Gender, race, and age were analyzed to reveal connections that may exist with cyberbullying activity. Cyberbullying literature varies on findings related to gender and engagement in cyberbullying activity. Hinduja and Patchin (2009) and Williams and Guerra (2007) reported that there were no significant differences in offending or victimization by gender, while Li (2007) found that females were more likely to be victims but that gender did not have a significant relationship in victimization in his study (Li, 2006). Ybarra and Mitchell (2007) found that boys were three times more likely than girls to be frequent perpetrators of online harassment. Dempsey et al. (2009) also found that females were more likely to be victims of cyberbullying than males, and males were more likely to report overt victimization. In this study the quantitative results from statistical analysis show that males are more likely to engage in cyberbullying activity as both perpetrators and victims.

However, the qualitative results of this study produced findings which were much to the contrary, with students indicating that the focus of cyberbullying was most often about females, except in the case of males who had their sexual identity questioned. This unexpected finding indicates that student perceptions regarding victimization differs markedly from the majority of the extant literature (Hinduja & Patchin, 2009; Li, 2006; Li 2007; Williams & Guerra, 2007) and the quantitative results of this study. These results concur with Dempsey et al. (2009) and are consistent with theories regarding relational and social traditional bullying where females are more likely to take part in indirect forms of bullying such as spreading rumors and engaging in social exclusion. It also concurs with the research results reported by Dowell, Burgess, and Cavanaugh (2009) who found that girls spent significantly more time on the Internet during a typical week, had significantly more email addresses, and used instant messaging significantly more than boys. All of these activities would give girls more time and tools to be cyberbullied with or use to cyberbully others. More research must be conducted on interactive video game play, in which more males mentioned taking part, and instances of cyberbullying in order to gain a deeper understanding of gender differences regarding cyberbullying behavior.

Few studies have looked at race as a factor in cyberbullying engagement. Hinduja and Patchin (2009) and Williams and Guerra (2007) found that there were no significant differences in offending or victimization by race in their respective studies. Results from the quantitative portion of this study indicate that African Americans were more likely to commit cyberbullying acts and be victimized by cyberbullying acts than whites. In qualitative focus groups the issue of race as it relates to cyberbullying did not emerge—perhaps because, like the metropolitan area, the schools were reflective of the somewhat homogenous nature of the different neighborhoods in which the schools were located. Some schools that were visited were also in lower-income communities. Regardless of gender, race and age the students participating in the study all had access to social technology. Therefore, if there is a digital divide with respect to cyberbullying, it is more of a participatory divide where lower-income students access social technology such as Facebook either at school, on their family's shared computer, or on the phone they may share with a sibling. Students, in this case, may not have immediate access to the information that social technology provided at home, but they had access to it throughout their day.

Hinduja and Patchin (2007) found that older youth were likely to be more engaged in cyberbullying activity than younger youth. Ybarra and Mitchell (2007) also reported that as the frequency of online harassment increases age tends to increase as well. This observation suggests that perhaps older students are utilizing social technology for social types of cyberbullying. However, Williams and Guerra (2007) surveyed students in grades 5, 8, and 11 (n=2,293) in Colorado and found that Internet bullying appeared to peak in middle school and then decline in high school. The quantitative aspect of this study found that older students are more likely to commit acts of cyberbullying on younger students, and that age was not statistically significant in predicting victimization. This finding is at odds with the qualitative data collected where middle school students indicated that the older middle school students and high school students indicated that younger high school students—especially freshmen—were more likely than upper classmen to be involved in cyberbullying behavior. However, younger middle school students and older high school students told stories about their same-aged friends being involved in cyberbullying activity as well. The data collected leads to the conclusion that cyberbullying acts may increase as students are gaining access (e.g., getting cell phones, getting their own laptop, starting to use Facebook) to the social technology tools and decrease as the students mature into their junior and senior years. However, as some situations arise such as rumors and gossip throughout their middle and high school careers, these situations often trigger cyberbullying acts.

Risky Behaviors and School Safety

Researchers have hypothesized connections between being a cyberbully and/or a cyberbully victim and engaging in risky behaviors such as alcohol and cigarette use (Bailey, 2008; Hinduja & Patchin, 2007; Hinduja & Patchin, 2009; Patchin & Hinduja, 2006; Mason, 2008; McGuinness, 2007) but few studies have empirically tested this connection empirically. This research study examined relationships between engaging in cyberbullying activity and other risky behaviors such as marijuana, prescription, and hard drug use. A majority of students that were surveyed reported not smoking cigarettes (92%), drinking (80%), smoking marijuana (83.5%), misusing prescription medications (89.5%), or partaking in hard drugs (94.7%). However, a few students did report taking part in some of these activities at an extremely high level with 3.1% smoking marijuana more than 40 times over the past month, 1.2% abusing prescription medications more than 40 times in their lifetime, and .9% partaking in hard drugs in the last year. Some students reported mild to moderate use of these substances. Further statistical analysis yielded cyberbullying victims and perpetrators having a significant relationship (.001) with smoking cigarettes, drinking alcohol, and abusing drugs. This finding is consistent with the research literature, and alerts researchers to the need to include the use of cigarettes, alcohol, and illegal drugs in cyberbullying prevention programs.

School safety was also a focus of this study. Disagreement is present in the literature insofar as Varjas et al. (2009) found that students did not equate school safety to acts of cyberbullying whereas Juvonen and Gross (2008) found that 60% of cyberbullying victims retaliated on school grounds and 28% retaliated *both* online and at school. Survey results in this study revealed that 16% of students were harassed, picked on, or bullied to the extent that they felt unsafe at school over the past 12 months. Some students indicated that their perception of safety affected their choice to attend school, with 15% reporting that they had missed school and 5% indicating that they brought a weapon to school. This is especially worrisome given that 15% reported fighting on school grounds at least once in the past 12 months. Further statistical analysis showed that the frequency of fighting, weapons, and prevalence of violence had a significant relationship at a .001 level with both cyberbullying victims and perpetrators.

Focus group sessions with middle and high school students demonstrated that rumors, gossip, and fights that started in school could carry over online to social network sites, and that the reverse was also true—that rumors, gossip, and fights that started online could carry over onto school grounds. This is due to the "friends" that students add to their social network accounts. Consistent with boyd (2008) and Ito et al. (2010), students were mostly friends with others that they knew. However, it did not take a close bond to add another person as a friend; instead, students were likely to add friends of friends, people they had met once at an event, and everyone at school whether they were close or not. Adding everyone at school gives students access to learn and push out information regarding themselves and others to a large audience in a short period of time. This provides ample space for cyberbullying perpetration and victimization. Students revealed that participation in bullying behavior—whether it be online or face-to-face—breeds more bullying activity due to the reciprocal nature of the online/face-to-face crossover, and the likelihood of the initial victim to retaliate.

Students had mixed responses when it came to cyberbullying and school safety. Like Varjas et al. (2009) they, for the most part, perceived their school environments as safe, but were aware of the crossover of cyberbullying acts. Many students thought that cyberbullying was just as serious (if not more serious) than traditional bullying as it had the potential to get spread throughout a large audience quickly. A few students also told stories about the sometime life-altering consequences of cyberbullying such as transferring schools and physical and online threats contributing to the murder of a family member. The lack of equating cyberbullying and school safety may be due to the nature of the students we spoke to or may be part of a larger problem of understanding what cyberbullying actually is and what the term encompasses.

Student Perceptions of Cyberbullying

When students were asked what cyberbullying was, they often answered initially with a canned response of "bullying over the Internet." When pushed to elaborate, students described how it took place and gave different examples they had witnessed, but they struggled to produce a clear, detailed definition that described what the act actually encompassed. A high school student said that cyberbullying was not a term they used, and instead suggested a more inclusive term; "talking smack" as being more appropriate. While talking smack may include threats to one's physical safety, it focuses more on spreading gossip and malicious rumors. Findings from this study indicate that students spread gossip and rumors both in person during school and hanging out with friends, as well as by using social technologies—especially Facebook and texting. However, not all students thought that gossip and rumors were necessarily any kind of bullying. Instead, it was something that happened daily and was part of the socializing scene.

Conceptualization and operationalization issues continue to persist among researchers. These issues are mimicked in our middle and high school student audiences as well. Without having a common understanding of what cyberbullying is, it becomes difficult to gain an accurate understanding of how it affects our nation's students. Also, a common terminology is needed for prevention and intervention programs that will resonate with students. While students may have been unclear on exactly what the cyberbullying act involved and did not involve, they reported that it was just as serious, if not more so, than traditional bullying alone. They indicated that the inability to see another's face makes it easy to get out of hand by going too far without knowing it, and that the medium sometimes gives courage to those who would not do harm to another in person.

The students that participated in the focus group sessions shared their own experiences with cyberbullying. Similar to Patchin and Hinduja (2006) who found that 47% witnessed an act of cyberbullying, many students in this study reported not engaging directly in the behavior but having often witnessed it occurring many students spoke of getting involved by defending their friends or family. Students shared both minor and major experiences about their own, their friends', or their family's engagement in cyberbullying activity. Minor cyberbullying incidents (e.g., a friend saying you were a bad friend) resulted in feeling anxious about how people viewed them, having hurt feelings about what was said, and feeling bad about oneself. These minor incident results were consistent with the traditional bullying literature which has indicated that victims tend to worry about the future and suffer self-doubts (Berthold & Hoover, 2000; Boynton-Jarrett et al., 2008). The extant cyberbullying literature also suggests that cyberbullying is associated with increased anxiety and lowered self-esteem (Dempsey et al., 2009; Juvonen & Gross, 2008; Mason, 2008; Willard, 2006).

Students did attribute adverse consequences to major incidents arising from cyberbullying. Major incidents involved students having to close their Facebook accounts, transfer to other schools, and receiving threats to physical safety. In one case, the combination of a series of cyberbullying and traditional bullying acts resulted in a student participant's relative being shot and killed. In the open-ended questionnaire students reported feeling sad about being victimized by cyberbullying perpetrators, but not to the point where they would take their own lives. However, it is possible that the constant hurt feelings, lowered self-esteem, and potential threats to one's safety could take a toll on students and lead them to thoughts of harming themselves. However, this is mere conjecture and much more research is needed about those individuals who are cyberbullied weekly and daily.

Students were very good about describing where cyberbullying typically takes place. They revealed that there was a reciprocal nature to cyberbullying in two respects. First, cyberbullying is reciprocal due to the overlap of Facebook friend networks and school environments. A rumor or piece of gossip that is spread in person among friends at school can end up on Facebook that evening, and the reverse is also true—a rumor or piece of gossip can be posted on Facebook after school and end up in school the next day. The second reciprocal aspect is the nature of cyberbullies and cyberbully victims as shown in Figure 2.

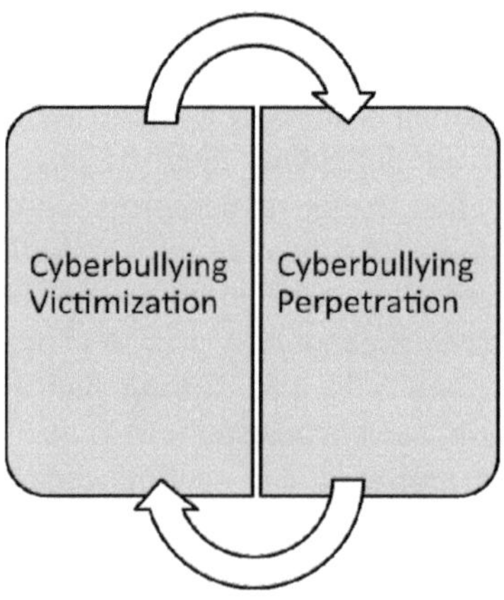

***Figure 2.* Reciprocal Nature of Cyberbullying. This figure illustrates the reciprocal nature of cyberbullying victimization and perpetration.**

A number of students revealed that students were often both perpetrators and victims because of retaliation and acts of revenge. If a rumor was posted about a student, that student might post something in retaliation. One of the scariest comments in the study came from a female middle school student who said that if she was cyberbullied she "would come back ten times harder."

According to students the major portion of the physical interaction in cyberbullying takes place at school—either during the school day (e.g., in class or during off periods) or at school events (e.g., talent shows). Where online cyberbullying takes place is a little more complex. It can happen while a student is at their house or a house of a friend. While it can take place over any of the social technology tools frequented by students, it mostly occurs over tools that are frequently used as a whole among the student population such as texting and Facebook. However, students also noted that cyberbullying occurs to a limited extant via instant messengers and emails. Facebook was mentioned the most as being the place that harbors cyberbullying activity.

This major role played by Facebook is likely due to the different facets available to cyberbullying perpetrators. Facebook allows cyberbullying users to create groups that make fun of others, post status messages talking badly about someone (but not always using their name), post messages to a victim's wall, or uploading a video aimed at hurting the victim. As many students have Facebook accounts, are "friends" with a majority of their fellow students, and check their account often when school is not in session, it also allows for access to an instant, attentive audience. Also, after posting a message making fun of another student in an individual act of cyberbullying, other students can pile on that initial comment further making fun of that student, thereby creating a group cyberbullying experience.

Mixing Quantitative and Qualitative Data

One of the study's research questions asked "to what extent and in what ways do qualitative data collection (i.e., focus groups and open-ended survey questions) among middle and high school students serve to contribute to a more comprehensive understanding of social technology use and cyberbullying for middle and high school students?" Mixed methods research is an appropriate methodological choice if it is the suitable way to answer the research questions posed (Tashakkori & Teddlie, 2003) and when neither the qualitative nor quantitative approach alone cannot adequately address the research problem (Creswell, 2009). This study's research questions focused on frequency, characteristics, relationships, and perceptions of cyberbullying, a topic which closely lends itself to a mixed methods approach. While results from the quantitative data analysis provided breadth (Tashakkori & Teddlie, 2003) by providing results from over 3,000 middle and high school students to reveal information regarding frequency (e.g., perpetration, victimization, etc.), characteristics (e.g., gender, age, race, etc.), and relationships (e.g., cyberbullying engagement with risky behaviors, violence, school safety) it was the qualitative data that provided depth in insight (Tashakkori & Teddlie, 2003) by gathering perceptions from middle and high school students and staff regarding the cyberbullying phenomenon.

These perceptions validate the quantitative aspect of the study by giving further explanation and elaborating on the initial findings (Creswell, 2009; Creswell, Clark, Gutmann, & Hanson, 2003; Johnson, Onwuegbuzie, & Turner, 2007), as well as disentangling intricate relationships (Sosulski & Lawrence, 2008) and bringing to light insights that might not otherwise be apparent (Bryman, 2007). For example, while the survey data revealed that 11% of students had been cyberbullied over the past year, it was the focus group and open-ended questionnaire qualitative data that permitted the explanation of the intricacies of the phenomenon. This qualitative data indicated which social technologies were used in cyberbullying activity, the role gossip and rumors play in student lives and cyberbullying activity, how school overlaps with social technology, and how students deal with cyberbullying victimization.

A few notable discrepancies arose from the two sets of data that may not have been seen if both quantitative and qualitative aspects were not included and viewed collectively. The first was in respect to gender regarding perpetration and victimization. The quantitative aspect indicated that males were more likely to be both victims and perpetrators of cyberbullying. The qualitative aspect, however, revealed that students perceived cyberbullying was usually about females—except in cases where a male's sexuality was in question—and could be perpetrated by females or males alike. Besides gender, quantitative and qualitative findings were at odds in regards to age. Quantitative results showed that older students were more likely to commit cyberbullying acts and that age was not significant in victimization. Qualitative results, in contrast, revealed that students perceived older middle school students (e.g., 8th graders) and younger high school students (9th and 10th graders) as being the most involved in the cyberbullying phenomenon.

This is connected to and leads to the third discrepancy, which revolves around what students perceive cyberbullying to actually be.

Frequency statistics revealed that 11% of students were victims of cyberbullying activity over the past year, which was lower than some current literature. Given that students were unsure of how to define what cyberbullying was and was not, this leads to an interesting conceptual dilemma. If spreading gossip and rumors would have been added to the survey, perhaps the frequency results may have been higher. Including quantitative survey results, qualitative focus groups, and qualitative open-ended questionnaire results brought to light complexities that emerged from the findings from multiple data sets that reveal helpful insights for future research. Further, both sets of data worked to validate the other, and created a more comprehensive picture of the cyberbullying phenomenon than if only one or the other had been conducted.

LIMITATIONS

Although a number of potentially important findings emerged from this analysis, this study has a number of limitations which must be noted in consideration of the results. As the quantitative and qualitative data collection processes occurred separately, limitations regarding these independent aspects will be discussed below. This section concludes with a consideration of the limitations regarding the mixed methodology approach.

Quantitative Data

While many interesting findings were uncovered in the quantitative data analysis, there are several important validity and reliability limitations that must be noted. First, while self-report survey data provided researchers with valuable information regarding cyberbullying perpetrators, victims, and incidents that may not be reported to schools or police, self-report data has some inherent limitations. Self-report survey data may be subject to recall error, the fabricating of offenses, or not indicating participation in offenses. This is especially true when questions are related to illegal or otherwise prohibited behavior (Maxfield & Babbie, 2009). In this case, students may have not remembered when a cyberbullying situation took place, or correctly recall how many times they had been a victim or perpetrator over a given amount of time. They may have also fabricated participation in offenses to intentionally skew results if they were averse to taking the survey in the first place. Because participants took part in this survey in school—even though they were promised confidentiality—they may have been intimidated to mark responses that were illegal (e.g., drug, alcohol, and cigarette use) or that were prohibited by the school (e.g., weapons, fighting, bullying, cyberbullying) thinking that perhaps a school staff member would gain access to their answers.

Further, it is important to note this was a secondary analysis of an existing data set. The data were gathered via a survey instrument that was edited by the initial researchers for their own research purposes (i.e., specific to risky behaviors that have an impact on the school environment). In that study, the YRBS was attached to an existing project which required annual survey administration. Some school district administrators and many individual schools balked at the annual administration of a lengthy survey. In order to substantially reduce the burden on schools, a shortened form of the YRBS was constructed yielding a single version of the survey questionnaire (for both middle and high schools). The 23 questions on the condensed instrument assessed the following constructs: demographics, perceptions of safety, fighting, bullying victimization, drug use and the perceived risk of drug use. Reliability analysis was conducted on the YRBS questions. Cronbach's alpha is .605 and the Cronbach's Alpha based on standardized items is .606.

While the questions suited the purpose of the initial researchers, a number of questions (e.g., depression, suicide, academic performance, etc.) were omitted from the original YRBS that would have been useful in this analysis. Initial researchers also edited the YRBS by adding three questions regarding social technology use and cyberbullying without piloting the new questions. The question asking students if they had been a victim of cyberbullying activity did not give examples of cyberbullying. It has become evident through this study that researchers, adults, and students do not see cyberbullying in the same ways and tend to define it somewhat differently. To derive a comprehensive understanding of cyberbullying frequency further research must be performed to determine student definitions of cyberbullying and then these definitions must be used in survey instruments. Findings from this study regarding race should also take into account that the survey instrument allowed students to select multiple responses when designating race. While this gives students the opportunity to select the different parts of their race, it makes calculating meaningful responses in this category difficult.

Finally, there were a total of 26 schools involved—representing a mix of public, private, and charter—which took part in the quantitative aspect of this study. The sample was not random, and its aim was to survey as many middle and high school students as possible from the *Safe Schools and Healthy Students Program*, which itself involves a portion of the schools in the research location. Thus, this study is not based on a representative sample of middle and high school students in the research location or the United States, and consequently cannot be generalized to a larger entity than those that are indicative of the program. Rather, it pertains to the perspectives of a large number of middle and high school students who attend schools that participated in the Safe Schools Healthy Choices Initiative in the research location in 2009. The survey data were gathered by schools on a voluntary basis. Thus, there may be a self-selection bias associated with the study's participating schools. Given the cross-sectional nature of the data collection and the potential self-selection bias, the generalizability of these findings is clearly limited. One should use caution in generalizing these findings to other urban student populations. However, an asset of this data set is that it provides responses from a large number of middle and high school students regarding engagement in risky and cyberbullying behavior; in fact, this data set provides the largest number of responses of any cyberbullying study conducted at the time of this study.

Qualitative Data

The qualitative aspect of this study provided many interesting student perceptions regarding cyberbullying activity, but as with the quantitative aspect of the study, it is not without its own limitations. According to Creswell (2008), qualitative inquiry's intent is not to generalize or hypothesize to a population, but rather to develop an in-depth exploration of a central phenomenon. To gain this in-depth knowledge, participants with experience with cyberbullying as a perpetrator, victim, or witness were purposely selected to share their perceptions regarding the activity. Due to the limited time, resources, and school response, only three schools agreed to provide a total of four student focus groups, one school staff focus group, and two school staff interviews. One school had not participated in the quantitative survey but wanted to participate in the qualitative aspect. This was allowed due to the lack of other schools' interest and because of the lapse in time between quantitative and qualitative data collection. This lapse could have resulted in different student populations for the focus groups compared to the survey. Also, in qualitative data collection the main focus was gathering student perceptions of cyberbullying-related matter. As a consequence of these several factors, study results cannot be generalized to a larger population. However, a comprehensive description of the participant focus groups and the sessions are provided to help the readers ascertain how closely the study situation matches their situation, and determine whether the results can be transferred (Merriam, 1998). Further, as this study was conducted cross-sectionally, information was limited to one point of time and can not reveal longitudinal trends.

In order to ensure that the results of the qualitative aspect of this study were trustworthy, transcripts were checked for accuracy, the focus group moderators examined findings through peer debriefing, and external researchers viewed the results. Also, a detailed account of positive, negative, and sometimes contradictory findings was presented. By providing a detailed account of the participants' experiences when writing the results, thick description was utilized so that the readers can naturalistically generalize their experiences to those that have been captured in the study (Denzin, 1989). Through thick description facets of social technology use and information regarding cyberbullying (e.g., the conceptualization disconnect, the role of rumors and gossip, etc.) emerged. These facets further described how students interacted while using social technologies. As an avid user of social technology, I also acknowledge the role my insider knowledge has played both in designing the study and in analyzing the results.

Mixed Methods Design

As this study utilized a previously collected quantitative data set in its design, it is important to note the discrepancy in data collection dates. A cross-sectional survey was distributed to middle and high school students who attended schools that participated in the *Safe Schools and Healthy Students Program* during February and March 2009. Student focus groups and staff interviews were conducted in April, May, and

June of 2011. As is the case with an experimental or quasi-experimental study, a sequential explanatory mixed method design with a lapse in time between quantitative and qualitative data collection may suffer some threats to internal validity. For example, historical events and events in students' lives may have occurred after the quantitative survey data collection and before the qualitative focus group sessions that could have altered the way students viewed cyberbullying.

In addition, students who participated in focus group sessions in 2011 may not have been the same individuals that took the YRBS in 2009 due to the expanse in time and logistics given particular school participation. Therefore, the quantitative YRBS results and the qualitative focus group data are seen as complimentary to one another and not necessarily arising from the same data pool. The contiguous nature of these data sets, as opposed to a single continuous data set, produces interpretation limitations and reduces internal validity. The findings of the two data sets, however, have implications for cyberbullying policy and literature.

SIGNIFICANCE OF FINDINGS AND STUDY IMPLICATIONS

Middle and high school students provided information regarding the cyberbullying phenomenon via the YRBS and focus groups. Middle and high school staff also spoke about their perceptions regarding cyberbullying activity through focus groups and interview sessions. While it is important to have an understanding of the key findings it is also essential to discuss the significance of these findings and their implications for youth and schools as they deal with cyberbullying.

What Can Youth Take Away from this Study?

Middle and high school students offered many interesting insights into cyberbullying through participating in the survey and focus group sessions. Quantitative data revealed that a few students endure intense victimization on a weekly or daily basis. It is important for youth to understand that cyberbullying happens frequently, and to know that they are not alone in their victimization. It is also important for students to understand the role that gossip and rumors play in cyberbullying and bullying activity generally. Students indicated that they were often connected to virtually all their classmates through social technology tools such as Facebook. While having this connection can make one feel like they belong to a group and are connected to people at large, it can also have ramifications in that it can perpetuate the game of telephone and passing along "smack," gossip, and malicious rumors. Advocating for students to not friend their school classmates would be much like advocating for students who are cyberbullied to just not go on Facebook or use texting. Instead, we advocate for enhanced student awareness in terms of whom they trust with their secrets and information. Students also need to be more careful about what they post and consider the ramifications of their posts. It is important that teenagers learn to treat others the way they want to be treated and develop empathy. While we advocate for this approach at an individual and school-wide level, to benefit victimized youth on a larger scale a cyberbullying website should be launched.

Sadly, current websites on cyberbullying tend to push out useful information to students and adults but fail to provide a "safe" place for at risk students. To reach students effectively, an interactive site would be necessary. This site would have relevant information for victims and those seeking to learn more about cyberbullying. It would also provide a message board for victims to connect with one another. The site might feature a chat option where a cyberbullying victim could anonymously chat via text, audio, or video messenger with a licensed counselor who has experience with cyberbullying and bullying behavior. In order for a strategy such as this to be effective, middle and high school students as well as licensed counselors and school staff would need to be involved in the conceptualization, design, and maintenance phases of the cyberbullying website.

In some cases, there is a reciprocal relationship in that victims lash out online and/or in person in retaliation against the perpetrators, thus the victims become cyberbullies and bullies themselves. In order for students to gain the understanding of the reciprocal nature of cyberbullying schools should offer information presentations; these will be discussed at length in the next section. One of the most interesting elements shared by students during the focus group sessions were their strategies for dealing with cyberbullying. Students spoke of both passive and active techniques for responding to a cyberbullying perpetrator. Passive techniques included not putting your trust in the wrong people by telling everyone your secrets, ignoring the activity, being happy with who you are, and when friends were cyberbullied to not get involved in acts of defensive retaliation. Active techniques included addressing the situation right away, confronting the perpetrator at school, telling someone, and defending yourself or your friends. While the active strategies bring the situation forward and may clear the air between individuals more quickly, they may also further escalate the scenario which may lead to verbal and physical altercations in school (e.g., during classes, during class breaks, before/after school).

With student perspective in mind and rather little research available addressing intervention tactics, researchers and school staff may advocate for a three-point cyberbullying approach as evidenced in Figure 3.

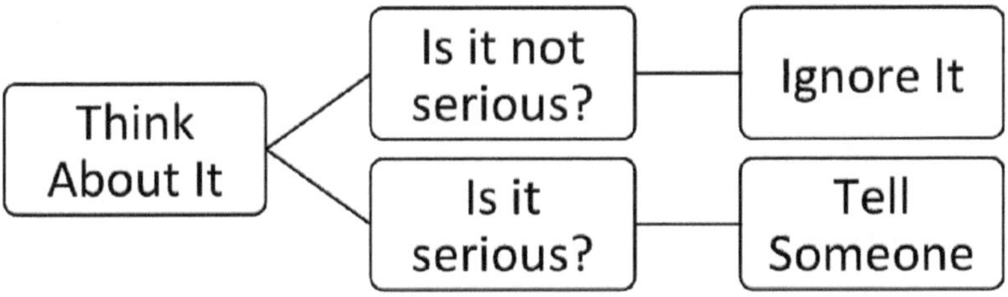

Figure 3. **Three-Point Approach. This figure illustrates a three-point approach to reacting when victimized by cyberbullying.**

This approach would first ask students to think about the situation and to determine the magnitude of the situation. If it is something minor, such as someone calling you a name you do not like or spreading a rumor about you that is obviously not true, then do nothing to further perpetuate the behavior or draw attention to yourself. If it is something more serious, tell someone like an older sibling or a parent if the student is not comfortable engaging the school staff in the issue. While much can be said for confronting issues directly, advocating for that approach will leave some students ill-equipped in a cycle of bullying behavior, as evidenced by the reciprocal nature of cyberbullying victimization and perpetration. Instead, this approach is student-centered and minimalist in regards to further confrontation between the perpetrator and victim. While the "tell someone" avenue may lead to the perpetrator and victim talking out their differences, it would have to be with parents or school personnel present. Parents and school personnel generally have some conflict resolution experience and could aptly supervise these situations. However, it is imperative that potential tactics such as these are vetted and tested exhaustively.

What Can Schools Take Away from this Study?

Middle and high school staff also shared their thoughts and perspectives regarding cyberbullying. This feedback, coupled with student responses, provides valuable insight regarding how cyberbullying affects students and the school environment. YRBS results reveal that some students feel unsafe at school and some are bringing weapons into the school environment. Further, cyberbullying activity—as a perpetrator or victim—is significantly related to engaging in drugs, violence, and traditional bullying behavior. Since cyberbullying is connected to violence and traditional bullying behavior, it is important that school staff acknowledge the relationship between the school environment and the after-school environment that takes place through texting and websites such as Facebook. There is little doubt that incidents that begin on Facebook result in conflict between individuals at school. Since some students are bringing weapons to school, these Facebook and face-to-face incidents may contribute to an already volatile situation.

Pursuant to these findings, schools need to focus on a combination of policy, prevention, and intervention tactics as show in Figure 4.

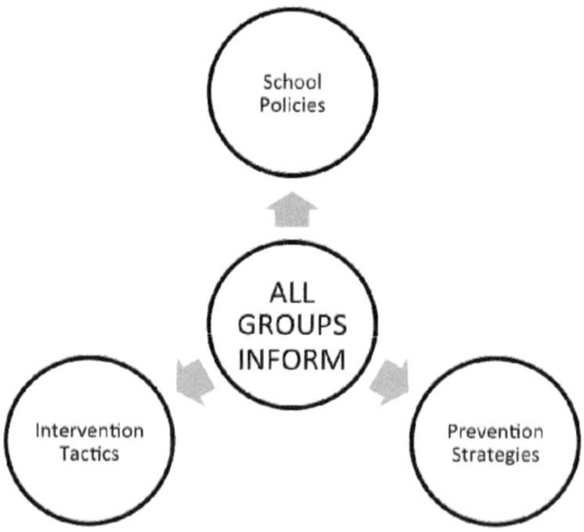

***Figure 4*. Tactics to Combat Cyberbullying. This figure illustrates the three major tactics to combat cyberbullying among youth.**

First, it is important that schools have policy in place which provides jurisdiction to act, thereby enabling schools to maintain student safety. An effective strategy is a written code of conduct depicting appropriate behavior at school and out of school—especially when engaging with one another using social technologies. While this is easier for a private school to accomplish, public schools may want to acknowledge the overlap between the school and after-school online environments in their school policies depicting appropriate behavior both in and out of school.

Second, it is important for schools to provide prevention services to their student body regarding cyberbullying victimization and perpetration. These services include adjusting the school structure to utilize block schedules, thereby minimizing unsupervised time when switching classes and decreasing the time allotted for lunch. While this may give students less time to confront one another in person, the opportunity still exists before or after school. Also, the problems that originate or worsen in cyberspace are still present. It is, therefore, important to reach students with a presentation series that starts at the beginning of the school year and repeats in small refreshers throughout the year. To be effective, the presentation would need to be interactive, with the presenter giving facts but also utilizing interactive questioning, small group activities, and large group discussion to get students involved and interested through an active learning pedagogy. Students may benefit from the following elements:

- Reviewing real cyberbullying stories
- Defining cyberbullying
- Deciphering where cyberbullying takes place
- Discussing why people cyberbully others
- Understanding how cyberbullying affects victims
- Brainstorming strategies to combat victimization
- Deliberating consequences of combatting victimization
- Examining strategies related to staying safe while using social technologies

To provide more detailed information regarding aspects of the presentation, it should catch the audience's attention by providing real stories of how cyberbullying has affected victims. These could range from minor consequences like stressed relationships and anxiety to grievous outcomes like violence and suicide.

A key element of the presentation would be to produce a definition of cyberbullying. This may be accomplished by asking students to define it in a large group, with prompts if necessary. After developing a group definition, it would be beneficial to follow with a small group activity that focuses on students applying that definition to a situation they may have seen in the past (e.g., a text making fun of someone that is overweight, a Facebook post about a rumor about a person's sexuality, or a vague status that is clearly about another schoolmate).

It would also be important to discuss where cyberbullying takes place (anytime/any place, through texts/Facebook, the face-to-face/online overlap). Points of view from both sides of the cyberbullying phenomenon (perpetrator and victims) should be discussed as well. To provide multiple viewpoints, the presenter would focus on why perpetrators commit acts of cyberbullying (jealousy, low self-esteem, stress relief) and how these acts effect victims (problems at school, problems with self). Also, the use of alcohol, cigarettes, and drugs as well as the reciprocal nature of being a cyberbully and a cyberbullying victim should be discussed.

An important aspect of the presentation would be to discuss with students how to handle cyberbullying situations. As a student-centered presentation, it is essential to get students to discuss potential responses to cyberbullying occurrences (i.e., what if someone said something mean to them on Facebook or via text, what if you saw two friends fighting on Facebook, what if you thought you or a friend was in danger because of a text or Facebook message). The presenter would highlight beneficial strategies mentioned by students and advocate for the three-point approach noted previously, which focuses on thinking about the situation and deciding on the seriousness of the situation. If it is a minor situation (e.g., calling someone a name), it is best to ignore it and not to engage with the cyberbully. If it was deemed to be a major situation (e.g., a threat to physical safety) it may be appropriate to tell someone. The key is to emphasize that posting in response or posting a separate message as retaliation often makes the situation worse.

School staff indicated a need for Internet safety training. An element of this presentation would include both general Internet and Facebook safety. General Internet safety items would include why students should protect themselves, the concept of public vs. private information, and not giving out information that allows people to locate you. Facebook safety items would include thinking about what you post, not being easy to track (not having your address/phone number/year you were born on your profile), and checking privacy settings often. This portion of the presentation would be accompanied by a demonstration of settings in the "My Account" section of Facebook, which includes who can see your information, who can search for you, who can send you messages, and who sees the information that you post.

An addition to a presentation series would be a monthly retreat with a focus on students getting to know one another. As a student indicated after a focus group session, a retreat should not be just limited to seniors as a fun goodbye activity—it could have value in people getting to know each other. In seeing commonalities, students may focus on them instead of fixating on differences, spreading rumors, and generating malicious gossip.

Finally, it is important for schools to provide intervention services when cyberbullying occurs. Schools must have a policy presenting a protocol for school staff actions when a cyberbullying situation is brought to their attention. While these policies and protocols are necessary, they also create a split in student trust as the students understand that teachers and school staff are required to take certain actions. Several school staff members described a specific, and effective, approach. First, they isolate involved students to gather information on the problematic situation. Next, they employ a mediation approach which allows students to advocate for themselves. While students noted trust issues regarding teachers and staff, those persons play an important role in mitigating cyberbullying.

It is important to acknowledge that school policies, prevention strategies, and intervention protocols should not be developed in a vacuum. Instead, it is important to include administrators, teachers, guidance counselors, students, parents, law enforcement, researchers, and leaders in the community (e.g., coaches, clergy, etc.) in developing these different, but equally important, components. Each of these parties view cyberbullying differently due to their experiences and every perspective should be valued in the pursuit to create healthy, safe spaces for youth.

Recommendations for Future Research

This study revealed a number of areas that need future research including the impact of technology on the way we interact with one another, how we think, and how we accomplish tasks. The concepts of public and private information are evolving due to people's constant access to others via social technology like Facebook. The way we take in knowledge is lending more to the length of blog posts and less to multi-page articles. Distractions—like music sites, sports sites, entertainment sites, and Facebook—make their way into the process of completing tasks, and multitasking has become a commonality among our population. These changes warrant study—especially as to how they affect our educational environments. More specifically regarding the cyberbullying phenomenon, we need to study if a constant access to peer networks via social technologies creates more instances of bullying or just extends what was already occurring. Gossip and rumors are going to be part of any middle school or high school—especially in regards to important things (e.g., promiscuity, sexuality, appearance, material possessions) to a teenage population who are coming of age, trying to define their identity, and who they want to be. Therefore, it is important to further study the role of gossip and rumors in cyberbullying activity and gain an understanding of how to get students to see how detrimental the spreading of rumors and gossip can be to the victims involved.

While this study began to determine possible intervention and prevention strategies, the tactics offered are only preliminary in nature. More research must be done to understand the usefulness of current school policies as well as if the other intervention and prevention strategies offered in this study work to decrease cyberbullying activity in schools. Another important area for continued research is to further conceptualize cyberbullying. Currently, there is a discrepancy between researchers, practitioners, and students regarding what cyberbullying truly is. Researchers must work with students to conceptualize the phenomenon and begin to define it in a way all parties recognize and understand. It is also necessary to look at how intense victimization (weekly, daily) impacts students both while in school and as an adult.

Finally, the most important area for future research is to longitudinally study groups of middle and high school students to gain an understanding of how cyberbullying engagement (as a perpetrator and/or victim) impacts school performance, psyche, self-esteem, depression, and participation in violent (e.g. fighting in school, bringing weapons to school) and risky (e.g., smoking cigarettes, drinking alcohol, and taking drugs) behaviors. A longitudinal study would also provide information regarding how cyberbullying engagement impacts their life as an adult.

CONCLUDING REMARKS

This study indicates that a majority of students do not intend to be cyberbullies. Therefore, we do not think that students that perpetrate cyberbullying acts are "bad" kids. Instead, we note the nature and frequency of student interactions, both within and outside of school. Some of these interactions create conflict scenarios. Depending on situational variables (e.g., how public is the post or text, who is involved, the kind of information posted, size of audience), it may escalate into something quite serious.

Gossip and rumors, like in previous generations, play a large part in the lives of middle and high school students and play pivotal roles in bullying and cyberbullying. Unfortunately, students do not always view gossip and rumors as being harmful or as bullying/cyberbullying and have difficulty explaining what constitutes cyberbullying behavior. Students have many more ways to share gossip, spread rumors, and lash out at each other than in the past. What was once limited to friends passing information in the hallways, at lunch, and over the phone can now spread instantly to huge numbers of people through texting or Facebook. The landscape of social technology is quickly changing. Texting and Facebook will soon become yesterday's mediums of choice and will be replaced with something new. Thus, it is not just about the specific kind technology—instead it is about youth, their interactions with one another, and the tools (right at that particular moment) they use to connect.

Solutions for cyberbullying are more complex than just asking parents to take away computer or cell phone privileges. In some homes, parents are at a disadvantage as they may not understand technology as well as their children or, they might have limited English skills. Taking away computers or cell phones to stop cyberbullying activity also limits students' ability to connect with others, further isolating them. As cyberbullying research evolves, more research is needed regarding effective solutions. Students need to gain more of an understanding of how cyberbullying impacts victims. Schools not only need to have codes of conduct that cover student behavior both in school and when using social technologies, they also need prevention strategies that define cyberbullying, produce an understanding of how cyberbullying happens, and how cyberbullying effects those involved. Retreats where students get to know each other and introduce commonalities may also decrease cyberbullying activity. The countless news stories, the limited literature around this phenomenon, and this study show that cyberbullying is an issue in our nation's schools. Cyberbullying needs more attention from researchers and strategies to combat this phenomenon need to be both fully conceptualized, developed, and measured.

Appendix A: Youth Risk Behavior Survey Questionnaire

Safe Schools/Healthy Students YRBS Questions

This survey is about health behavior. It has been developed so you can tell us what you do that may affect your health. The information you give will be used to develop better health education for young people like yourself.

Your name will not be on this survey. The answers you give will be kept private. No one will know what you answer. Answer the questions based on what you really do.

Completing the survey is voluntary. Whether or not you answer the questions will not affect your grade in this class. If you are not comfortable answering a question, just leave it blank.

The questions that ask about your background will be used only to describe the types of students completing this survey. The information will not be used to find out your name. No names will ever be reported.

Make sure to read every question. When you are finished, follow the instructions of the person giving you the survey.

Thank you very much for your help.

1. Please write your four-digit school identification code in the "Special Codes" section on the answer sheet and darken the corresponding circles.

2. Please write the name of your school in the "Last Name" and "First Name" section on the answer sheet and darken the corresponding circles.

3. How old are you?
   (0) 12 years old or younger
   (1) 13 years old
   (2) 14 years old
   (3) 15 years old
   (4) 16 years old
   (5) 17 years old
   (6) 18 years old or older

4. What grade are you in?
   (0) 6th grade
   (1) 7th grade
   (2) 8th grade
   (3) 9th grade
   (4) 10th grade
   (5) 11th grade
   (6) 12th grade

5. What is your sex?
   (0) Female
   (1) Male

6. Are you Hispanic or Latino?
   (0) Yes
   (1) No

7. What is your race? **(Select one or more responses)**
   (0) American Indian or Alaska Native
   (1) Asian
   (2) Black or African American
   (3) Native Hawaiian or Other Pacific Islander
   (4) White

8. During the past 30 days, on how many days did you **not** go to school because you felt you would be unsafe at school or on your way to or from school?
(0) 0 days
(1) 1 day
(2) 2 or 3 days
(3) 4 or 5 days
(4) 6 or more days

9. During the past 12 months, how many times were you in a physical fight **on school property?**
(0) 0 times
(1) 1 time
(2) 2 or 3 times
(3) 4 or 5 times
(4) 6 or 7 times
(5) 8 or 9 times
(6) 10 or 11 times
(7) 12 or more times

10. During the past 12 months, have you been harassed, picked on, or bullied so much that you felt unsafe at school?
(0) Yes
(1) No
(2) Not Sure

11. Do you agree or disagree that violence is a problem at your school?
(0) Strongly agree
(1) Agree
(2) Not sure
(3) Disagree
(4) Strongly disagree

12. During the past 30 days, on how many days did you carry a weapon such as a gun, knife or club **on school property?**
(0) 0 days
(1) 1 day
(2) 2 or 3 days
(3) 4 or 5 days
(4) 6 or more days

13. During the past 30 days, on how many days did you smoke cigarettes?
(0) 0 days
(1) 1 or 2 days
(2) 3 to 5 days
(3) 6 to 9 days
(4) 10 to 19 days
(5) 20 to 29 days
(6) all 30 days

14. How much do you think people risk harming themselves (physically or in other ways) if they smoke one or more packs of cigarettes per day?
(0) No risk
(1) Slight risk
(2) Moderate risk
(3) Great risk

15. During the past 30 days, on how many days did you have at least one drink of alcohol?
(0) 0 days
(1) 1 or 2 days
(2) 3 to 5 days
(3) 6 to 9 days
(4) 10 to 19 days
(5) 20 to 29 days
(6) all 30 days

16. How much do you think people risk harming themselves (physically and in other ways) if they take one or two drinks of alcohol nearly every day?
(0) No risk
(1) Slight risk
(2) Moderate risk
(3) Great risk

17. During the past 30 days, how many times did you use marijuana?
(0) 0 times
(1) 1 or 2 times
(2) 3 to 9 times
(3) 10 to 19 times
(4) 20 to 39 times
(5) 40 or more time

18. During your life, how many times have you taken a **prescription drug**, such as OxyContin, Percocet, Vicodin, Ritalin or Xanax without a doctor's prescription?
(0) 0 times
(1) 1 or 2 times
(2) 3 to 9 times
(3) 10 to 19 times
(4) 20 to 39 times
(5) 40 or more times

19. During the past 12 months, how many times did you use cocaine, crack, methamphetamines, ecstasy or heroin?
(0) 0 times
(1) 1 or 2 times
(2) 3 to 9 times
(3) 10 to 19 times
(4) 20 to 39 times
(5) 40 or more times

20. During the past 12 months, has anyone offered, sold or given you an illegal drug **on school property?**
(0) Yes
(1) No

21. How often do you use MySpace.com, Facebook.com, chat rooms or other online social networking websites?
(0) Never
(1) A few times per year
(2) A few times per month
(3) A few times per week, each week
(4) Every day

22. How often have you been the victim of cyber-bullying in a chat room or social networking website such as MySpace.com or Facebook.com?
(0) Never
(1) A few times per year
(2) A few times per month
(3) A few times per week, each week
(4) Every day

23. How often do you make fun of or tell lies about other students using email, instant messaging or social networking websites such as MySpace.com or Facebook.com?
(0) Never
(1) A few times per year
(2) A few times per month
(3) A few times per week, each week
(4) Every day

Thank you for completing the survey.

Appendix B: Student Focus Group Protocol

General Welcome (5 minutes)

1. Introduce Myself

2. Focus Group Purpose
    a. To gather information regarding social technology use (i.e., texting, social networks, instant messaging, email, etc.) and related behaviors

3. Focus Group Boundaries and Expectations
    a. Length of time
        i. 40-45 minute group discussion
        ii. 15 minute follow-up, open-ended questionnaire period
    b. Ethical considerations
        i. Voluntary
        ii. Confidential
    c. Boundaries
        i. If something is too personal, don't feel pressured to share—that is what the open-ended questionnaire is for if you would like to share that information
        ii. Always treat people the way you want to be treated
            1. Listen when other people are talking
            2. Don't interrupt others—wait until they are done
            3. Things people share are confidential and shouldn't be shared outside the walls of the focus group

Warm-Ups (5-10 minutes)

1. Introductions
   a. Name
   b. Favorite thing to do online
   c. One interesting thing about yourself

Basic Social Technology Use Background (10-15 minutes)

1. Which social communication technologies—like texting, instant messaging, and social networking sites—do you use to communicate with others?
   a. Prompts:
      i. How many times on an average day do you text?
      ii. How many times on an average day do you use instant messengers?
      iii. How many times on an average day do you use email?
      iv. How many times on an average day do you use social networking sites?

2. How do you use different social communication technologies to communicate with others? Are there specific features you use or don't use?
   a. Prompts:
      i. Which features of social networking sites do you use? Photos? Wall?

3. Do you use different social communication technologies to communicate with different people?
   a. Prompts:
      i. Who do you email?
      ii. Who do you instant message?
      iii. Whose wall do you write on?

4. Do you use social communication technologies to communicate with those you know (i.e., close friends, acquaintances, family, etc.) or those you don't know (i.e., people you just meet online)?
    a. Prompts:
        i. Do you use chat rooms? If so, is it with people you know face-to-face or just those that you've met online?
        ii. Which technologies do you use to meet new people?

5. Do you use social communication technologies to communicate with your friends and schoolmates after you go home from school? If so, why do you communicate with them after school and what technologies do you use?
    a. Prompts:
        i. Communicate to hangout virtually when bored?
        ii. Set plans up for face-to-face meetings?

Cyberbullying (10-15 minutes)

1. How familiar are you with cyberbullying?
    a. Prompts:
        i. Have you heard of any stories in the media? What do you think of these stories?

2. How often do you think cyberbullying happens?
    a. Prompts:
        i. Often, not that often

3. Where does most of the cyberbullying happen?
    a. Prompts:
        i. At home or school?
        ii. Through texting?
        iii. Through social network sites?
        iv. Through instant messaging?
        v. Through websites or bashboards?
        vi. Through email?

4. What forms can cyberbullying take?
    a. Prompts:
        i. Stealing passwords and altering sites, contacting friends/masquerading?
        ii. Posting mean messages or threats?

5. Who does most of the cyberbullying?
    a. Prompts:
        i. People you know or people you don't know?
        ii. Groups, individuals, or both?

6. How do you think that cyberbullying impacts the school environment?
    a. Prompts:
        i. Does it make it hard for victims to come to school?
        ii. Does it make it hard for victims to concentrate at school?
        iii. Do people take the cyberbullying into the physical school environment?

7. How would you define cyberbullying?
    a. Prompts:
        i. Does it need a power differential (someone able to manipulate or have an understanding of technology)?
        ii. Does it need to be repetitive? How do you define whether something is repetitive or not? Is it just posted once? What about shared more than once?
        iii. Does it need intent to harm behind it?
        iv. Are any of these components necessary? (perhaps share with them a commonly held definition and see if they agree or disagree)

8. How do people deal with cyberbullying?
    a. Prompts:
        i. Tell a friend?
        ii. Tell an adult?
        iii. Shut the computer or phone off?

Cyberbullying and Risky Behaviors (10 minutes) Individual Questionnaire

1. Give instructions to the follow-up, open-ended questionnaire
    a. Do not put your name on it—it is anonymous
    b. Please feel free to share as much or as little as you feel comfortable with
    c. The purpose of this is to help get a better understanding of cyberbullying

Conclusion (5 minutes)

1. Thank you for participating

2. Remember, respect and boundaries.

3. Give them a handout of where they can turn to if they need help (i.e., links to cyberbullying & risky behavior [school safety, school violence, alcohol, drugs, etc.] resources

Appendix C: Follow-up, Open-ended Questionnaire

Cyberbullying and Risky Behaviors

Directions: Please read and comment on the following questions carefully. Remember that your answers are anonymous.

1. Have you ever used social communication technologies like email, social networking sites, and instant messengers to cyberbully another individual? If so, why? Please describe your experience.

2. Have you ever been a victim of cyberbullying? If so, can you please describe your experience? How did it make you feel? How did you deal with situation—what tactics did you use?

3. Have you ever not gone to school or not wanted to go to school because you've been involved in a cyberbullying incident? If so, what about the cyberbullying made you not want to go to school?

4. Has a cyberbullying incident ever made you carry a weapon to school? If so, please describe your experience.
5. Has a cyberbullying incident ever created a problem for you at school? If so, please describe your experience.

6. Has a cyberbullying experience ever played a role in you using alcoholic beverages, tobacco products, prescription, or illegal drugs? If so, please describe your experience.

7. Has a cyberbullying experience ever left you feeling depressed or contemplating suicide? If so, please describe your experience.

Appendix D: School Staff Focus Group and Interview Questions

Basic Social Technology Use

1. Which social communication technologies (e.g., texting, instant messaging, social networking sites) do you see teenagers using to communicate with one another?

2. Does the school allow use of these technologies in school?

3. How familiar are you and your colleagues with these technologies?

4. What are your biggest problems when it comes to these social communication technologies?

Cyberbullying

1. How familiar are you with cyberbullying?

2. How would you define cyberbullying? What forms can it take?

3. How often does it occur? Does it happen more than it gets reported?

4. What is your biggest concern related to cyberbullying?

Cyberbullying and the School Environment

1. How do you think cyberbullying impacts students? Do students involved have a tough time concentrating when they're involved in a cyberbullying incident? Do students that engage in cyberbullying participate in other risky behaviors (e.g., drinking, drugs, weapons, etc.)?

2. How does cyberbullying impact the school environment? Do students get into fights at school as a result of something that begins on Facebook?

3. What do students tend to fight about on Facebook?

4. What does the school do when they learn of a case of cyberbullying? What are your limitations?

5. How does school staff intervene to monitor communication via Facebook? Are fake profiles made? Do teachers become "friends" with students?

6. Do you have any prevention programs? If so, can you tell me more about them? If not, what do you think would help curtail cyberbullying?

References

Agatston, P., Kowalski, R., & Limber, S. (2007). Student perspectives on cyber bullying. *Journal of Adolescent Health, 41*, S59-S60.

Allen, K.P. (2012). Off the radar and ubiquitous: Text messaging and its relationship to 'drama' and cyberbullying in an affluent, academically rigorous US high school. *Journal of Youth Studies, 15*(1), 99-117.

American Medical Association. (2002, May 3). Youth bullying. Proceedings: Educational Forum on Adolescent Health. Chicago, IL: American Medical Association.

Bailey, L. (2008). bullying. *State Legislatures, October/November*, 23-25.

Barker, V. (2009). Older adolescents' motivations for social network site use: The influence of gender, group identity, and collective self-esteem. *CyberPsychology & Behavior, 12*(2), 209-213.

Bazeley, P. (2002). Issues in mixing qualitative and quantitative approaches to research. In R. Buber, J. Gadner, & L. Richards (Eds.), *Applying qualitative methods to marketing management research*. UK: Palgrave Machmillian, 141-156.

Beran, T. & Li, Q. (2007). The relationship between cyberbullying and school bullying. *Journal of Student Wellbeing, 1*(2), 15-33.

Berthold, K., & Hoover, J. (2000). Correlates of bullying and victimization among intermediate students in the midwestern USA. *School Psychology International, 21*(1), 65-78.

Bian, J., Agichtein, E., Liu, Y, & Zha, H. (2008, April). Finding the right facts in the crowd: Factoid question answering over social media. *International World Wide Web Conference*, Beijing, China.

Boyd, d. (2007a). Social networked sites: Public, private, or what? *Knowledge Tree 13*, May.

Boyd, d. (2007b). Why youth (heart) social networking sites: The role of networked publics in teenage social life. *MacArthur Series on Digital Learning—Youth, Identity, and Digital Media Volume (ed. David Buckingham)*. Cambridge, MA: MIT Press.

Boyd, d. (2007c). Socializing digitally. *Vodafone Receiver Magazine, 18: The Home*, June.

Boyd, d. (2007d). The significance of social software. *BlogTalks Reloaded: Social Software Research & Cases* (eds.) Thomas N. Burg and Jan Schmidt. Norderstedt, 15-30.

Boyd, d. (2008). Taken out of context: American teen sociality in networked publics. Ph.D. Dissertation. University of California-Berkeley, School of Information.

Boyd, d., & Ellison, N.B. (2007). Social network sites: Definition, history, and scholarship. *Journal of Computer-Mediated Communication, 13*(1), article 11.

Boynton-Jarrett, R., Ryan, L., Berkman, L., & Wright, R. (2008). Cumulative violence exposure and self-rated health: Longitudinal study of adolescents in the United States. *Pediatrics, 122*(5), 961-970.

Bradley, A. (2010, January 7). A new definition of social media. *Gartner Blog Network*. Retrieved from: http://blogs.gartner.com/anthony_bradley/2010/01/07/a-new-definition-of-social-media/

Bradshaw, C.P., Waasdorp, T.E., & O'Brennan, L.M. (2013). Teachers' and education support professionals' perspectives on bullying and prevention: Findings from a national education association study. *School Psychology Review, 42*(3), 280-297.

Brener, N.D., Collins, J.L., Kann, L., Warren, C.W., Williams, B.I. (1995). Reliability of the youth risk behavior survey questionnaire. *American Journal of Epidemiology, 141*: 675– 80.

Bryman, A. (2007). Barriers to integrating quantitative and qualitative research. *Journal of Mixed Methods Research, 1*(1), 8-22.

Campbell, M.A., Slee, P.T., Spears, B., Butler, D., & Kift, S. (2013). Do cyberbullies suffer too? Cyberbullies' perceptions of the harm they cause to others and to their own mental health. *School Psychology International, 34*(6), 613-629.

Coyle, C.L., & Vaughn, H. (2008). Social networking: Communication revolution or evolution? *Bell Labs Technical Journal, 13*(2), 13-18.

Creswell, J.W. (2008). *Educational research: Planning, conducting, and evaluating quantitative and qualitative research* (3rd ed.). Upper Saddle River, NJ: Pearson.

Creswell, J.W. (2009). *Research design: Qualitative, quantitative, and mixed methods approaches* (3rd ed.). Los Angeles, CA: Sage.

Creswell, J.W., Clark, V.L., Gutmann, M.L., & Hanson, W.E. (2003).

Advanced mixed methods designs. In A. Tashakkori & C. Teddlie (Eds.), *Handbook of mixed methods in social & behavioral research* (pp. 209-240). Thousand Oaks, CA: Sage.

Dake, Price, & Telljohann (2003). The Nature and extent of bullying at school. *Journal of School Health, 73*(5), 173-180.

Dempsey, A.G., Sulkowski, M. L., Nichols, R. & Storch, E.A. (2009). Differences between peer victimization in cyber and physical settings and associated psychosocial adjustment in early adolescence. *Psychology in the Schools, 46*(10), 962-972.

Digital_nation: life on the virtual frontier. (2010). *PBS.* Retrieved from: http://www.pbs.org/wgbh/pages/frontline/digitalnation/

Denscombe, M. (2008). Communities of practice: A research paradigm for the mixed methods approach. *Journal of Mixed Methods Research, 2*(3), 270-283.

Dooley, J.J., Pyzalski, J. & Cross, D. (2009). Cyberbullying versus face-to-face bullying: A theoretical and conceptual review. *Journal of Psychology, 217*(4): 182-188.

Dowell, E.B., Burgess, A.W., & Cavanaugh, D.J. (2009). Clustering of internet risk behaviors in a middle school student population. *Journal of School Health, 79*: 547-553.

Fredrick, K. (2009). Mean girls (and boys): Cyberbullying and what can be done about It. *School Library Media Activities Monthly, 25*(8), 44-45.

Gravetter, F.J. & Wallnau, L.B. (2007). *Statistics for the behavioral sciences*. Belmont, CA: Thompson Learning.

Greene, J.C. (2008). Is mixed methods social inquiry a distinctive methodology? *Journal of Mixed Methods Research, 2*(1), 7-22.

Harris, S. & Petrie, G.F. (2003). *Bullying: The bullies, the victims, and the bystanders*. Lanham, MD: Rowman & Littlefield Publishing.

Heary, C.M. & Hennessy, E. (2002). The use of focus group interviews in pediatric health care research. *Journal of Pediatric Psychology, 27* (1), 47-57.

Hinduja, S. & Patchin, J. (2007). Offline consequences of online victimization: School violence and delinquency. *Journal of School Violence, 6*(3), 89-112.

Hinduja, S., & Patchin, J. (2008). Cyberbullying: An exploratory analysis of factors related to offending and victimization. *Deviant Behavior, 29*(2), 129-156.

Hinduja, S. & Patchin, J. (2009). *Bullying beyond the schoolyard:*

Preventing and responding to cyberbullying. Thousand Oaks: Corwin Press.

Hinduja, S. & Patchin, J. (2010a). Bullying, cyberbullying, and suicide. Archives of Suicide Research, 14, 206-221.

Hinduja, S. & Patchin, J. (2010b). *Research.* Cyberbullying Research Center. Retrieved from: http://www.cyberbullying.us/research.php.

Hinduja, S. & Patchin, J. (2013). Social influences of cyberbullying behaviors among middle and high school students. *Journal of Youth Adolescence, 42*, 711-722.

Horner, S.D. (2000). Focus on research methods: Using focus group methods with middle school children. *Research in Nursing & Health, 23*, 510-517.

Ito, M., Horst, H., Bittani, M, boyd, d., Herr-Stephanson, B., Lange, P.G., . . . Robinson, L. (2008, November). Living and learning with new media: Summary of findings from the digital youth project. *The John D. and Catherine T. MacArthur Foundation Reports on Digital Media and Learning*. Retrieved from: http://www.macfound.org/atf/cf/%7BB0386CE3-8B29-4162-8098-E466FB856794%7D/DML_ETHNOG_WHITEPAPER.PDF

Ito, M., Baumer, S., Bittani, M., boyd, d., Cody, R., Herr-Stephanson, B., . . . Trip, L. (2010). *Hanging out, messing around, and geeking out: Kids living and learning with new media*. Cambridge, MA: Massachusetts Institute of Technology.

Jackson, C. (2006). E-Bully. *Teaching Tolerance, 29*, 50-54.

Jang, E.E., McDougall, D.E., Pollon, D., Herbert, M., & Russell, P. (2008). Integrative mixed methods data analytic strategies in research on school success in challenging circumstances. *Journal of Mixed Methods Research, 2*(3), 221-247.

Johnson, R.B., & Onwuegbuzie, A.J. (2004). Mixed methods research: A research paradigm whose time has come. *Educational Researcher, 33*(7), 14-26.

Johnson, R.B., Onwuegbuzie, A.J., & Turner, L. (2007). Toward a definition of mixed methods research. *Journal of Mixed Methods Research, 1*(2), 112-133.

Juvonen, J., & Gross, E.F. (2008). Extending the school grounds?—Bullying experiences in cyberspace. *Journal of School Health, 78*(9): 496-505.

Kirchen, R. (2008, February 22). Mayfair mall's teen chaperone policy paying off. *The Business Journal of Milwaukee*. Retrieved from:

http://milwaukee.bizjournals.com/milwaukee/stories/2008/02/25/story2.html

Kowalski, R.M., & Limber, S.P. (2007). Electronic bullying among middle school students. *Journal of Adolescent Health, 41*, S22-S30.

Kowalski, R.M., Limber, S.P., & Agatston, P.W. (2008). *Cyberbullying: Bullying in the digital age*. Malden, MA: Blackwell Publishing.

Kowalksi, R.M., Morgan, C.A., & Limber, S.P. (2012). Traditional bullying as a potential warning sign of cyberbullying. *School Psychology International, 33*(5), 505-519.

Krueger, R. & Casey, M. (2000). *Focus groups: A practical guide for applied research* (3rd ed.). Thousand Oaks, CA: Sage.

Lenhart, A., Madden, M., Macgill, A., & Smith, A. (2007). Teens and social media. *Pew Internet & American Life Project*. Retrieved from: http://www.pewinternet.org/Reports/2007/Teens-and-Social-Media.aspx

Lenhart, A., Ling, R., Campbell, R., & Purcell, K. (2010). Teens and mobile phones. *Pew Internet & American Life Project*. Retrieved from: http://www.pewinternet.org/Reports/2010/Teens-and-Mobile-Phones.aspx

Lenhart, A., Purcell, K., Smith, A., & Zickhur, K. (2010). Social media & mobile internet use among teens and young adults. *Pew Internet & American Life Project*. Retrieved from: http://pewinternet.org/Reports/2010/Social□Media□and□Young□Adults.aspx

Lenhart, A., Madden, M., Smith, A., Purcell, K., Zickuhr, K., & Rainie, L. (2011). Teens, kindness, and cruelty on social network sites. *Pew Internet & American Life Project*. Retrieved from: http://www.pewinternet.org/2011/11/09/teens-kindness-and-cruelty-on-social-network-sites/

Li, Q. (2006). Cyberbullying in schools: A research of gender differences. *School Psychology International, 27*(2), 157-170.

Li, Q. (2007). New bottle but old wine: A research of cyberbullying in schools. *Computers in Human Behavior, 23*(4), 1777-1791.

Li, Q. (2008). A cross-cultural comparison of adolescents' experience related to cyberbullying. *Educational Research, 50*(3), 223-234.

Madden, M., Lenhart, A., Duggan, M., Cortesi, S., & Gasser, U.

(2013). Teens and technology 2013. *Pew Internet & American Life Project*. Retrieved from: http://www.pewinternet.org/2013/03/13/teens-and-technology-2013/

Mason, K. (2008). Cyberbullying: A preliminary assessment for school personnel. *Psychology in the Schools, 45*(4), 323-348.

Maxfield, M. & Babbie, E. (2009). *Basics of research methods for criminal justice and criminology* (2nd ed.). Belmont, CA: Wadsworth.

McGuinness, T.M. (2007). Dispelling the myths of bullying. *Journal of Psychosocial Nursing, 45*(10), 19-22.

Mishna, F., Saini, M., and Solomon, S. (2009). Ongoing and online: Children and youth's perceptions of cyber bullying. *Children and Youth Services Review, 31*, 1222-1228.

Mitchell, K.J., Finkelhor, D., & Wolak, J. (2004). Victimization of youths on the internet. In J.L. Mullings, J.W. Marquart & D.J. Hartley (Eds.) *The Victimization of Children: Emerging Issues*. (pp. 1-39). New York, NY: The Haworth Maltreatment & Trauma Press.

Morse, J.M. (2003). Principles of mixed methods research designs. In A. Tashakkori & C. Teddlie (Eds.), *Handbook of mixed methods in social & behavioral research* (pp. 189-208). Thousand Oaks, CA: Sage.

Nansel, T., Overpeck, M., Pilla, R., Ruan, W., Simons-Morton, B., & Scheidt, P. (2001). Bullying behaviors among U.S. youth: Prevalence and association with psychosocial adjustment. *JAMA, 285 (16)*, 2094-2100.

Nations, C. (n.d.). What is social media? What are social media sites? *About.com Webtrends*. Retrieved from: http://webtrends.about.com/od/web20/a/social-media.htm

North, S., Snyder, I., & Bulfin, S. (2008). Digital tastes: Social class and young people's technology use. *Information, Communication, & Society, 11*(7): 895-911.

Olweus, D. (1978). *Aggression in the schools: Bullies and whipping boys*. New York, NY: Hemisphere.

Olweus, D. (1993). *Bullying at school: What we know and what we can do*. Cambridge, MA: Blackwell.

Patchin, J., & Hinduja, S. (2006). Bullies move beyond the schoolyard:

A preliminary look at cyberbullying. *Youth Violence and Juvenile Justice, (2)*, 148-169.

Pieschl, S., Porsch, T., Kahl, T., & Klockenbusch, R. (2013). Relevant dimensions of cyberbullying—Results from two experimental studies. *Journal of Applied Developmental Psychology*, *34*, 241-252.

Porter, C.E. (2004). A typology of virtual communities: A multi-disciplinary foundation for future research. *Journal of Computer-Mediated Communication, 10*(1), article 3.

Raskauskas, J. & Stoltz, A.D. (2007). Involvement in traditional and electronic bullying among adolescents. *Developmental Psychology, 43*(3), 564-575.

Rosen, L.D., Cheever, N.A., & Carrier, M. (2008). The association of parenting style and child age with parental limit setting and adolescent MySpace behavior. *Journal of Applied Developmental Psychology, 29*: 459-471.

Rusby, J., Forrester, K., Biglan, A., & Metzler, C. (2005). Relationships between peer harassment and adolescent problem behaviors. *Journal of Early Adolescence, 25*(4), 453-477.

Sampson, R. (2009). Bullying in school. Community Oriented Policing Services. *U.S. Department of Justice*, 12.

Seals & Young (2003). Bullying and victimization: Prevalence and relationships to gender, grade level, ethnicity, self-esteem, and depression. *Adolescence, 38*(152), 735-47.

Sengupta, A. & Chaudhuri, A. (2011). Are social networking sites a source of online harassment for teens? Evidence from survey data. *Children and Youth Services Review, 33*, 284-290.

Smith, P., Morita, Y., Junger-Tas, J., Olweus, D., Catalano, R., & Slee, P. (1999). *The nature of school bullying : A cross-national perspective.* New York, NY: Routledge.

Smith, P., Mahdavi, J., Carvalho, M., Fisher, S., Russell, S., & Tippett, N. (2008). Cyberbullying: Its nature and impact in secondary school pupils. *Journal of Child Psychology & Psychiatry, 49*(4), 376-385.

Sosulski, M.R. & Lawrence, C. (2008). Mixing mixed methods for full-strength results: Two welfare studies. *Journal of Mixed Methods Research, 2*(2), 121-148.

Stover, D. (2006). Treating cyberbullying as a school violence issue.

Education Digest: Essential Readings Condensed for Quick Review, 72(4), 40-42.

Strom, P., & Strom, R. (2005). Cyberbullying by adolescents: A preliminary assessment. *The Educational Forum, 70*, 21-32.

Subrahmanyam, K., & Greenfield, P. (2008). Online communication and adolescent relationships. *Future of Children, 18*(1), 119-146.

Tashakkori, A. & Creswell, J.W. (2007). Editorial: Exploring the nature of research questions in mixed methods research. *Journal of Mixed Methods Research, 1*(3), 207-211.

Tashakkori, A. & Teddlie, C. (Eds.). (2003). *Handbook of mixed methods in social & behavioral research.* Thousand Oaks, CA: Sage.

Tharp-Taylor, S., Haviland, A., & D'Amico, E. (2009). Victimization from mental and physical bullying and substance use in early adolescence. *Addictive Behaviors, 34*(6/7), 561-567.

U.S. Census Bureau. (2010). State and county quick facts. Retrieved from: http://quickfacts.census.gov/qfd/states/55/55079.html.

U.S. Department of Health and Human Services. (2003). Bullying is not a fact of life. *Substance Abuse and Mental Services Administration*. Retrieved from: http://www.mentalhealth.org/publications/allpubs/SVP-0052/.

Vandebosch, H., & Van Cleemput, K. (2008). Defining Cyberbullying: A qualitative research into the perceptions of youngsters. *CyberPsychology & Behavior, 11*(4): 499-503.

Varjas, K., Henrich, C., & Meyers, J. (2009). Urban middle school students' perceptions of bullying, cyberbullying, and school safety. *Journal of School Violence, 8*(2), 159-176.

Wagner, C. (2008). Beating the cyberbullies: Targets of taunting need help turning the tables on tormentors. *The Futurist*, *42*(5), 14-15.

Watkins, S.C. (2009). *The young & the digital: What the migration to social-network sites, games, and anytime, anywhere media means for our future*. Boston, MA: Beacon Press.

Wellman, B., Salaff, J., Dimitrova, D., Garton, L., Gulia, M., & Haythornthwaite, C. (1996). Computer networks as social networks: Collaborative work, telework, and virtual community. *Annual Review of Sociology, 22*: 213-238.

Willard, N. (2006). Flame retardant: Cyberbullies torment their victims 24/7: Here's how to stop the abuse. *School Library Journal, 52*(4), 54.

Williams, K.R. & Guerra, N.G. (2007). Prevalence and predictors of internet bullying. *Journal of Adolescent Health, 41*, S14-S21.
Williams, A.L., & Merten, M.J. (2008). A review of online social networking profiles by adolescents: Implications for future research and intervention. *Adolescence, 43*(170), 253-274.
Williams, A.L, & Merten, M.J. (2009). Adolescents' online social networking following the death of a peer. *Journal of Adolescent Research, 24*(1), 67-90.
WiredKids. (nd). Wired safety. Retrieved from: http://wiredkids.org/.
Wolak, J., Mitchell, K.J., & Finkelhor, D. (2007). Does online harassment constitute bullying? An exploration of online harassment by known peers and online-only contacts. *Journal of Adolescent Health, 41*, S51-S58.
Wolfsberg, J. (2006). Student safety from cyberbullies, in chat rooms, and in instant messaging. *Education Digest: Essential Readings Condensed for Quick Review, 72*(2), 33-37.
Wolpert, S. (2005, March 28). Bullying among sixth graders a daily occurrence, UCLA study finds. UCLA Newsroom. Retrieved from: http://newsroom.ucla.edu/portal/ucla/Bullying-Among-Sixth-Graders-a-6006.aspx?RelNum=6006
Ybarra, M.L., & Mitchell, K.J. (2004). Online aggressor/targets, aggressors, and targets: A comparison of associated youth characteristics. *Journal of Child Psychology and Psychiatry, 45*(7), 1308-1316.
Ybarra, M.L., & Mitchell, K.J. (2007). Prevalence and frequency of internet harassment instigation: Implications for adolescent health. *Journal of Adolescent Health, 41*, 189-195.
Ybarra, M.L., Diener-West, M., & Leaf, P.J. (2007). Examining the overlap in internet harassment and school bullying: Implications for school intervention. *Journal of Adolescent Health, 41*, S42-S50.

Index

www.ingramcontent.com/pod-product-compliance
Ingram Content Group UK Ltd.
Pitfield, Milton Keynes, MK11 3LW, UK
UKHW041121071026
15587UKWH00009B/30

9 781593 327613